# The History of the Assyrian Nation In the 20<sup>th</sup> Century

## With Special Emphasis on the Events of World War I & World War II

By
Koorish Yacob Shlemon

Translated By
Arianne Ishaya Ph.D.

SEYFO Center Publications, 2022

www.seyfocenter.com

# In Memory of Ninos Aho

**Thank you!**

We would like to express our sincere gratitude to our supporters for their generous contributions to SEYFO Center as we work tirelessly to raise awareness regarding the history and genocide of the Assyrian people.

This publication would not have been possible without the support of our friends:

Sami Aturaya & Hanna Lazar
Emanuel and Ramona Goriel
Dr. Samir Johna, Without Borders

We would also like to thank Mr. Fred Isaac for his assistance in setting up the manuscript for the publication process.

# Table of Contents

## Chapter 15
World War II Its Impact on the Middle
Eastern countries especially

This book was written originally in the Assyrian language and was published by Nineveh Press in Chicago, in 1985.

Translator,

Arianne Ishaya

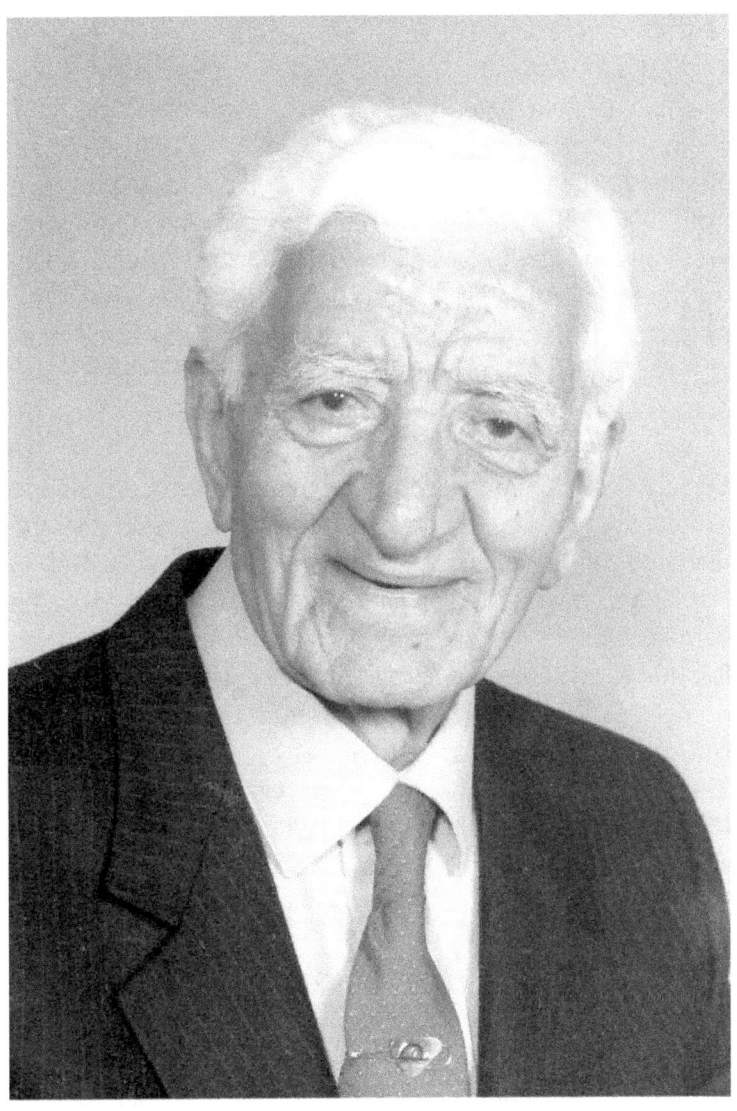

The Picture of the Author at the Age of 85

7

# The Biography of the Author:

Koorish is the son of Mr. Yacob Daniel from the lineage of "Bet shlimuni" of the village of Digala, in the district of Urmia, Iran. He was born in that village in 1900. From 1906-1913, he attended primary and secondary school in that village. Then from 1914-1918, he pursued his college education at the Urmia Presbyterian Mission college known as Qala-d-Sahabi" where the director was Dr. William Ambrose Shedd. Some well-known Assyrian instructors worked there together with some non-Assyrian language teachers who taught Farsi, French, Russian, and English.

On July 31, 1918, together with a large number of Assyrians and Armenians, we fled to the interior of the country in the direction of Sayen Qala and Hamadan. Upon arrival in Hamadan, I was enlisted in military service as a sergeant in the "Urmia Battalion" which was set up in Abshineh, near Hamadan for the purpose of liberating Urmia and other parts of our homeland. When we were transferred to Baquba refugee camp, I was promoted to the rank of a one-star officer. Shortly after moving to Mindan refugee camp which is 40 miles east of Mosul, we embarked on our first mission to Kurdistan on our way to liberate Urmia. This was on April 27, 1920, at which time I was promoted to the rank of a two-star officer.

After the necessary military preparations, we marched towards Kurdistan on October 21, 1920. But the mission was not successful. When the battalion returned to Mindan, the British dismantled the camp and I was released from military duty. My family and I returned to Baghdad in the spring of 1921. After a short stay in Baghdad, I found employment in the accounting office of the railway company and worked there until 1962.

Meanwhile, on Oct. 10, 1950, when Rev. Khando H. Yonan who was the pastor of the Evangelical Church and also the director of the school in Baghdad passed away, the duty of running the school and pastoring the church fell on my shoulders.

It was very difficult for me to run both the church and the school while holding a full-time job. But the Lord helped in that the company I was working for was sympathetic and gave me time off from work to fulfill my duties at the school and then return back to work.

From 1950-1965 we had different pastors, but from 1965-1973 our church was left without a pastor. Even though my health was frail, I conducted Sunday services and fulfilled other church-related duties during that time. But for official services such as weddings, funerals, and the Lord's Supper at which time an ordained pastor is required, I invited a Presbyterian pastor from Egypt who conducted services in Arabic.

I successfully served at the Church and managed the school until 1973 at which time my wife and I immigrated to the United States to join our son and daughters already there.

Up till this day we have lived in a large Assyrian community under the sovereignty of the almighty God and the leadership of this blessed country, the United States of America. We pray that the inhabitants of this country will whole-heartedly recognize God as the lord of their life.

In the end, it is important to note that in my 56 years of living in Iraq I gained knowledge in different aspects of life because I did not stay idle during my spare time. I have been diligent in reading the Holy Book and meditating on it; at the same time increasing my knowledge on other subjects pertaining to life. For all this, I am forever thankful to God.

# Dedication

I dedicate this book as a token of love and esteem to:

My wife Florence who has been a faithful life partner for 51 years beginning on the day of our wedding on February 5, 1934; to my eldest son Edwin and his wife Adeline; to our daughters Adaina and her husband Yoel, Adrina and her husband Sargon, and Anita and her husband William.

As well, to all the relatives, who have encouraged me to write a concise history of our people so that our sons and daughters today and all who will come after, will know about the centuries-old history of persecution and suffering of our nation.

Koorish Yacob Shlemon

# Preface:

## The History of a Fallen Nation, and Its Quest for a State After a Genocide

This book was written by Koorish Yacob Shlemon, who taught and led prayers at the Evangelical Church in Baghdad, Iraq over some parts of the second half of the twentieth century. Born near Urmia, Persia, in 1900, he lived through most of the Assyrians' twentieth century history, and received the encouragement of his friends and family to write a history of his time and his people. A postscript by Shamasha Gewargis d'bet Benyamin refers to its author as an eyewitness who could record the truth, a task for which the Assyrian people were indebted to him. In the new translation by Dr. Arianne Ishaya, Shamasha Benyamin writes that: "We have learned new, and unforgettable lessons that help us build a better future for the present Assyrians and those who will come after them."

The author writes that he was from the village of Digala, in the district of Urmia, being born in 1900. He describes being educated between 1914 and 1918 at the Urmia Presbyterian mission college under the mission's director, Dr. William Ambrose Shedd. Dr. Shedd wrote, of his role there, that it was a "post of honor to be occupied, a centre of incalculable influence to be filled, a people of enterprise and intelligence to be moulded by the gospel."[1]

The history of the Assyrian nation provided by the author covers Assyrian origins and Christianization, the history of Urmia in Persia, World War I, foreign missionaries' role in

---

[1]     American Board of Commissioners for Foreign Missions, Annual Report [Sixty-Second] (Boston: Riverside Press, 1872), 30-31.

Persia, the Assyrian Persians' exile in Hamadan and Baquba, the road to World War II in Kurdistan and the vicinity of Baghdad, and the Second World War's legacy and meaning for Middle Eastern peoples.

The initial scene of the action in Persia is vividly painted by the author. Three rivers meet in the Urmia region: "They have their source in the snowy mountains of Kurdistan and flow down into the Lake of Urmia. The first river is called Nazlu Chai and flows north of the town of Urmia. The second is centrally located and is called the Shahar Chai [The Town River]. The third is the Baranduz River in the south of the town." The lake was 30-40 miles wide and drew its name from the ancient Sumero-Akkadian "Ur" or city and "Mia" or water, terms which made their way into Old Assyrian and from there into Aramaic, the common language of the Assyrian Empire and subsequently the Persian Empire.

The author dedicates chapter 3 to the physical context of the story. He traces Urmia's name to "the cradle of water" in Assyrian. He describes the natural environment, the architecture and culture of the town and its surrounding villages, and the people. The author claims that 100,000 Assyrians lived in Persia when the First World War broke out, 70,000 Assyrians in the Urmia region and 30,000 in the suburbs/exurbs of Salamas and Sulduz. Other estimates differ, population registration frequently being linked to military service and to taxation.

This book addresses the Ottoman Christian genocide starting in chapter 4. He writes that the wartime conditions provoked a distress call from Christians everywhere they lived. The greatest catastrophe was that which occurred to our brothers the Armenians of Van and the surrounding villages where thousands were cruelly massacred by the Turks.

At this time Turkey officially entered the war on the side of Germany. Then Turkey spread propaganda in its newspapers and in other media of communication to the effect that Emperor Wilhelm of Germany strongly advocated the conversion of all inhabitants of Turkey to Islam. Of course, this was false news and had no basis in truth.

Following Abraham Yohannan and Gabriele Yonan, I have also studied the propaganda that led to genocide being perpetrated against the Armenians, Assyrians, Greeks, and even the Yezidis and some Jews of the Ottoman Empire. Dr. Yohannan, a Professor of Oriental Languages at Columbia University, wrote that Jevdet Bey, the son of the Ottoman military commander for the expedition to Persia, directed the war machine of the empire against the noncombatants of the Urmia region, particularly Salamas.[2] Yonan traced this campaign to German colonialist politics and orientalist theory prior to and during the war, which laid the groundwork for a total war in the eastern empire, including Christian extermination.[3] Some scholars have recently tried to downplay the German role, and I respond to them in a recent work.[4]

---

[2] *The Death of a Nation, or, the Ever Persecuted Nestorian or Assyrian Christians* (New York: G.P Putnam's Sons, 1916), 138.

[3] Gabriele Yonan, Ein vergessener Holocaust: Die Vernichtung der christlichen Assyrer in der Türkei (Göttingen: Gesellschaft für bedrohte Völker, 1989), 80-109.

[4] Hannibal Travis, "Responses to Genocide: Medieval Violence or Demographic Surgery as Moments in the Dialectics of Enlightenment," in A Cultural History of Genocide, Elisa von Joeden-Forgey ed. (London: Bloomsbury, 2021), 111-132.

There are also books that provide more details on the Assyrian genocides of 1914-1925 and 1932-1933.[5] One notable recognition came in 1918, when the U.S. Ambassador to the Ottoman Empire, Henry Morgenthau, recognized the "massacre[]" in the Ottoman Empire of "2,000,000 men, women, and children—Greeks, Assyrians, Armenians; fully 1,500,000 Armenians."[6] Another significant account appeared in 1935, with insights into how the Iraqi army and allied Kurdish leaders attacked the Assyrians of several districts in Iraq, and then committed massacres or occupied Assyrian communities.[7] Previously, a text possibly linked to the Church of the East via Mar Shimun Eshai was published.[8]

As the author notes, much of the prevailing narrative of the late 20th century was misleading by leaving out the Assyrians. Many people in what is today Iraq, Syria, and Turkey were Christian when the Arab conquest took place, having converted in large part from Assyro-Babylonian religious traditions associated with Nabu, Aššur, Ishtar, Shamash, Sin, etc. (The author makes this observation in chapter 2.)

The Assyrians lost their ancestral homes and churches in the Urmia region, the Hakkari mountains of present-day

---

[5]     Hannibal Travis, Genocide in the Middle East: The Ottoman Empire, Iraq, and Sudan (Durham, NC: Carolina Academic Press, 2010); "Assyrian Genocide," in Dictionary of Genocide, Vol. 1, Samuel Totten, Paul Robert Bartrop, and Steven L. Jacobs eds. (Westport, CT: Greenwood Publishing Group, 2008), 24-26.

[6]     "Morgenthau Urges Carving of Turkey," The Los Angeles Times, Dec. 12, 1918, p. I-1.

[7]     Lt. Col. Ronald S. Stafford, The Tragedy of the Assyrians (London: G. Allen & Unwin, Ltd., 1935). See also, Ernest Main, Iraq from Mandate to Independence (London: Kegan Paul, 1935).

[8]     The Assyrian Tragedy, (Annemasse, Switzerland: n.p., 1934).

14

southwestern Turkey, the vicinity of Diyarbakir and Mardin in today's Turkey, and in several districts in Iraq in which Assyrians had settled post-1918.[9] The Governor General of the Azerbaijan province of Persia wrote to the Prime Minister of Persia in 1919 to report that Kurds in Urmia "set about massacring some Assyrians," and then "sacked the villages of the environs, massacred the peasants and occupied all the shores of [Lake Urmia]."[10] Similarly, Armenians lost their communities and religious centers in present-day eastern Turkey, and Greeks fled their communities and religious centers both in the east of Turkey and in north-central Turkey (its Black Sea coast) and northwestern and far western Turkey (its Sea of Marmara and Aegean Sea coasts). After all this, the Treaty of Lausanne became known as a compendium of "moral horror[s]" from the Orthodox Christian point of view, even as it created many economic and colonial opportunities for the Americans, British, French, and Italians."[11]

---

[9]     Paul Shimmon, "Hakkiari," in The Treatment of Armenians in the Ottoman Empire, James Bryce and Arnold Toynbee eds. (London: Her Majesty's Stationery Office, 1916), 200–203; Lady Surma d'Bait Mar Shimun, "Refugees from Hakkiari," in The Treatment of Armenians in the Ottoman Empire, pp. 203-218. See also, Sargon Donabed, Reforging a Forgotten History: Iraq and the Assyrians in the 20th Century (Edinburgh: University of Edinburgh Press, 2015), 229-237, 278-342.

[10]    Travis, Genocide in the Middle East, 256.

[11]    Merrill D. Peterson, Starving Armenians: America and the Armenian Genocide, 1915-1930 and After (Charlottesville, VA: University of Virginia Press, 2004); 134-35; Hans Köchler, Global Justice or Global Revenge? International Criminal Justice at the Crossroads (New York, NY: Springer-Verlag, 2004): 58; Vahakn Dadrian, The History of the Armenian Genocide (New York: Berghahn Books, 1995), 333, 341; M. Cherif Bassiouni, "From Versailles to Rwanda in Seventy-Five Years: The Need to Establish a Permanent International Criminal Court," Harvard Human Rights Journal 10 (1997): 17.

The author provides unique insight into another period, the genocide perpetrated after the World War I armistice and Allied control of Istanbul, but before the Mosul Dispute was resolved. He writes:

In 1922 the tribes of Upper Tyari and Lower Tyari joined forces and returned to tribal lands and began to repair their houses and live in them. After 2-3 years the Turks sent a Vali [governor] accompanied by some soldiers to investigate why these people were living in the area without permission from the Turkish government. This is because this territory which was the ancestral home of our Ashirat brothers was now ceded to the Turks. Therefore, residence there without the knowledge of the Turkish government was not feasible.

Before the arrival of the Vali and his underlings in Tyari, the Tkhumnai had blocked their way and shot and wounded the Vali. They had also killed some of the soldiers. Then they had taken the Vali and his soldiers to Mosul to turn them over to the British. On the way, they had met Malik Khoshaba who set the Vali and his men free. The Vali went and reported the incident to the Turkish central government.

So, in 1924 Turkey sent an army against these Ashirats. The Ashirats were driven away from their homes a second time and had to return to Iraq.

Gabriele Yonan observed in 1989 that the Assyrian genocide had been forgotten, even though it had claimed more than 250,000 lives and emptied the Assyrian villages of Hakkari and the Urmia region, among other places.[12]

---

[12]    Gabriele Yonan, Ein vergessener Holocaust, op cit.

In 1999, Eden Naby and Michael Hopper gathered some essential documents and photographs concerning the Assyrian in an exhibit and published bibliography.[13] The early 2000s also saw significant works by the Assyrian Australian Academic Society, Joseph Alichoran, Donald Bloxham, Sebastian de Courtois, and Martin Tamcke that made the same point, tracing the genocide back to the 1890s in the case of de Courtois in particular.[14] Recognition of the Assyrian genocide by the European Parliament occurred in 2006, to be followed by the Swedish, Armenian, German, Austrian, and South Australian parliaments, as well as by the legislature of the State of California.[15]

---

[13]      Eden Naby and Michael E. Hopper (eds.), The Assyrian Experience: Sources for the Study of the 19th and 20th Centuries (Cambridge: Harvard College Library, 1999); Review of Middle East Studies 33, no. 2 (1999): 284.

[14]      The Assyrian Australian Academic Society, The Untold Holocaust (2000), www.youtube.com/watch?v=s2NGrRdlp2E; Donald Bloxham, The Great Game of Genocide: Imperialism, Nationalism and the Destruction of the Ottoman Armenians (Oxford University Press, 2005), 75, 97-98; Sébastien de Courtois, Le génocide oublié. Chrétiens d'Orient, les derniers Araméens (Paris: Ellipses, 2002); Sébastien de Courtois, The Forgotten Genocide: The Eastern Christians, The Last Arameans (Piscataway, NJ: Gorgias Press, 2004); Martin Tamcke, "Der Genozid an den Assyrern/Nestorianern," in Verfolgung, Vertreibung und Vernichtung der Christen im Osmanischen Reich 1912-1922 (Tessa Hofmann ed., LIT Verlag Munster, 2004), 109; Tessa Hofmann, "Mit einer Stimme sprechen – gegen Volkermord," in Verfolgung, Vertreibung und Vernichtung, 17-59; Jacques Rhétoré, « Les Chrétiens aux bêtes » Souvenirs de la guerre sainte proclamée par les Turcs contre les chrétiens en 1915 (Joseph Alichoran ed. and trans., Paris: Editions du Cerf, 2005); see also, Yves Ternon, Mardin 1915 : anatomie pathologique d'une destruction (Paris: Geuthner, 2007), http://www.imprescriptible.fr/rhac/tome4/.

[15]      European Parliament, "European Parliament Resolution on the Opening of Negotiations with Turkey" (Sept. 28, 2005), http://www.europarl.eu.int.

By 2004, some scholars who had previously written of the "Armenian genocide" mentioned Assyrians, correcting their work in the earlier period.[16] A frequent theme of such publications in the 2004-2014 period was the infliction of serious bodily and mental harm on Assyrians, in addition to the killings and child abductions that had been documented by Assyrian authors in the 1916-1946 period. In 2005, Katherine Derderian published an influential article entitled "Common Fate, Different Experience: Gender-Specific Aspects of the Armenian Genocide, 1915-1917" in Holocaust and Genocide Studies. In it, which she followed other scholars in adopting a narrative in which 1.5 million Armenians or more were killed and tens of thousands of Armenian women and children were raped and/or kidnapped by Turks and Kurds.[17] Her narrative omitted any reference to rapes of women or children of Assyrian or Greek race, even though her sources leave no doubt about this.[18] In 2018, Eden Naby corrected the record by gathering stories of Assyrian abductions as well, for publication in a volume which I edited.[19]

---

[16] Tessa Hofmann, "Mit einer Stimme sprechen – gegen Volkermord," in Verfolgung, Vertreibung und Vernichtung der Christen im Osmanischen Reich 1912-1922 (Tessa Hofmann ed., LIT Verlag Munster, 2004 and 2d ed. Münster, 2007), 109; Yves Ternon, Mardin 1915: Anatomie pathologique d'une destruction (Revue d'Histoire Arménienne Contemporaine, 2002), http://www.imprescriptible.fr/rhac/tome4/.

[17] Katherine Derderian, "Common Fate, Different Experience: Gender-Specific Aspects of the Armenian Genocide, 1915-1917," Holocaust and Genocide Studies.

[18] For example, one source, the Blue Book, mentions many abductions of Assyrians. Dr. Yohannan seems to have drawn on this source.

[19] Eden Naby, "Abduction, Rape, and Genocide: Urmia's Assyrian Girls and Women," in The Assyrian Genocide: Cultural and Political Legacies, Hannibal Travis ed. (Abingdon and New York: Routledge, 2018).

Previously, a scholar at the Massachusetts Institute of Technology's history department had written that "following its centuries-old tradition of pragmatism in domestic and foreign policy, the Ottoman ruling party, the Committee of Union and Progress (CUP), known as the Young Turks, created the conditions for, allowed, and openly encouraged Ottoman Muslim households (Turks, Kurds, Arabs, Circassians, Chechens, Gypsies, and émigrés from the Balkans) to incorporate Armenian women and children, and to a lesser extent those of other Christians groups such as Greeks and Assyrians."[20] Similarly, interview research with Assyro-Chaldean and Aramean descendants of Ottoman Christians who lived in Bote during the genocide revealed that rape and captivity were widespread.[21] Dr. Yohannan had also written of the local Kurds and Persian of the Urmia region taking Assyrian women captive, and abusing them.[22]

Thus, during what is commonly known as the Armenian Genocide, there were qualitatively and quantitatively similar genocides against the other Ottoman Christian populations, namely the Assyrians[23] and Greeks.[24] Books like this one may

---

[20]     Lerna Ekmekcioglu, "A Climate for Abduction, a Climate for Redemption: The Politics of Inclusion [sic] during and after the Armenian Genocide," Comparative Studies in and History 55, no. 3 (2013): 522-553, 526.

[21]     S. Mutlu-Numansen and Ringo Ossewaarde, "Heroines of Gendercide: The Religious Sensemaking of Rape and Abduction in Aramean, Assyrian and Chaldean Migrant Communities," European Journal of Women's Studies 22, no. 4 (2015): 428-442.

[22]     Death of a Nation, 139-46.

[23]     Assyrian is used here in reference to all of the Christian denominations linked to historic Assyria, and to the nineteenth century Christian Syrians (suraye, suraya, sureta, suroye, suryaya, suryoyo, etc.): the Chaldean rite, Church of the East, Assyrian Catholic, Assyrian Orthodox, Syrian Orthodox, Syrian Catholic, and "Syriac" Christians.

help alter the trajectory of scholarship and restore the earlier understanding that Ottoman Christians suffered as one.

The author concludes his text with the history of Assyrians in Iraq to 1958 and a sketch of the Assyrian Diaspora, amounting to some 400,000 persons on three continents, by his reckoning. The decisions taken at the Lausanne Conference and the meetings of the League of Nations dashed Assyrians' hopes to join the Arab kingdoms and constituent peoples of other former empires in exercising the right of self-governance. They lived under monarchy or military dictatorship in Iraq, Syria, Iran, and Turkey for many of the ensuing four decades. A postscript hopes that the lessons drawn from the experiences of Assyrians in flight from Persia to Iraq, some back to Persian (then Iran) and from there around the world, will inform Assyrians' future paths. Recent history, including the destruction of Turkey's institutions of democratic governance, the radicalization of the Iranian state since 2003, and the rise of the Islamic State of Iraq and Syria have shown that the Assyrians' lack of self-governance in their homeland may continue

Hannibal Travis
Professor, Florida International University

---

[24]    See generally The Genocide of the Christian Populations in the Ottoman Empire and Its Aftermath, Theodosius Kyriakidis and Kyrakos Chatzikyriakidis eds., (Abingdon and New York: Routledge, forthcoming 2022); Benny Morris and Dror Ze'evi, The Thirty-Year Genocide: Turkey's Destruction of Its Christian Minorities, 1894-1924 (Cambridge, MA, and London: Harvard University Press, 2019); Travis, Genocide in the Middle East; Joseph Yacoub, The Year of the Sword: The Assyrian Christian Genocide, a History (Oxford: Oxford University Press, 2016).

# Introduction

It was on my mind to write a short history of our nation from the turn of the 20th Century with a special focus on the events of World War I (1914-1918) and World War II (1939-1944). But for various reasons, this task was postponed until now.

Many friends have encouraged me to write a brief history of our people, which unfortunately is a sad one. Especially sad are the horrific events that took by storm those of us who lived in Urmia, Salamas, Targawar, Margawar, together with our tribal brothers in the mountains of Hakkari in Kurdistan during the two World Wars. The Wars culminated in the uprooting of our people and their exodus to Bet Nahrain, Iraq, and eventually to the immigration of some Assyrians to the blessed and prosperous country of the USA.

Note that it is not easy to compile and write a history that is both informative and interesting to the reader. Several conditions must be met. First, the author must have some knowledge of classical Syriac and be proficient in modern Swadai language to be able to convey his message accurately. Second, it is equally important to have adequate historical sources about major events, movements of people, pictures of famous personalities who have played a major role in the wars and political affairs during that period of time. Third, the author should make sure that the events he writes about are factual so that the careful reader will not find errors or stories which have no basis in truth.

Even though I am not claiming to have mastered all the above-mentioned skills, I am committed to fulfilling the task that is asked of me and relies heavily on the Lord to grant me time and wisdom to complete this work. My hope is that it will be factual, informative, and attractive to the reader.

My goal is to write this history in a simple Swadai language since it is used daily by our people and can be understood easily.

I have been a participant in a great many events during the historical period I write about. I have personal experiences and have witnessed events with my own eyes. But regarding those that have occurred far from me, I have gathered information through reliable books.

My final goal is to fulfill this duty so that it will be lasting memorabilia to our people especially to the generations after us and to those who have not known about the persecutions and suffering we have endured in the Near East and the Middle East for many centuries.

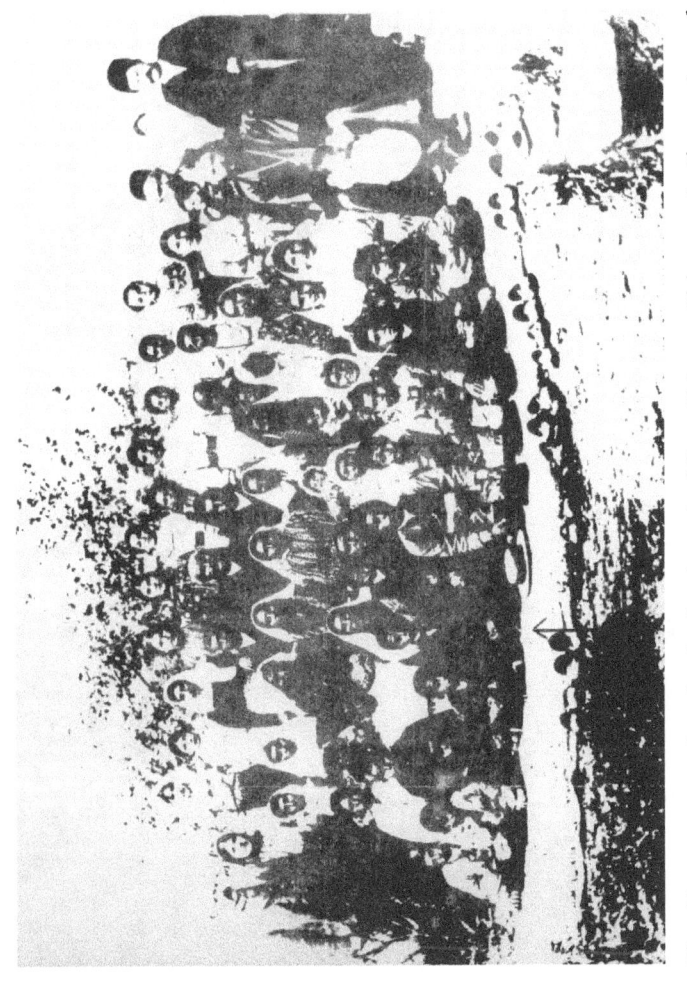

The Picture was taken in the backyard of Rev. Shimun Shlemon in the spring of 1908. This is the family of Bet Shlemons in Digala, Urmia. The author is 8 years old.

# 115 Assyrian Villages in Urmia, Iran

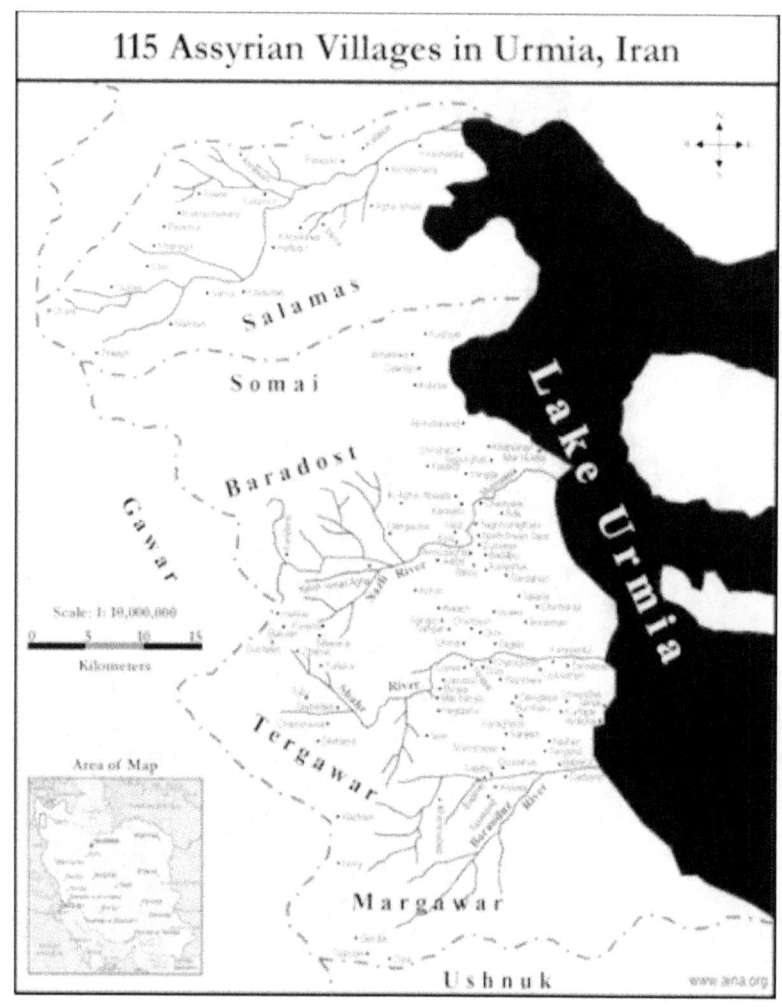

# Chapter 1
## Briefly,
## Who Are We and Where Are We From?

To begin with, I find it appropriate to comment very briefly on who we are, where we are from, and what is our true identity.

My goal here is not to rewrite the history of our ancient empire and the name of the great kings who ruled over a large territory in Asia Minor for 520 years that is, from 1228-708 B.C. The reader might say "We are tired of reading about these old stories that have been retold in different books by our writers." I am referring here to famous Assyrian writers such as Mirza David Malik, Rabi Eshaya-d-Shamasha David, Rabi Mushi Khanna-d-Chamakieh, Malik Yaccu-d-Malik Ismail of the Upper Tyari, Shamasha Gewargis Bet Benyamin-d-Ashita, Dr. Peera Sarmas, Girshun Duman, and other writers before me. They have all given us important and thorough historical accounts about our people.

As for me, I was prompted to write about the last 100 years history of our people especially in Urmia and surrounding villages with special emphasis on the persecutions and uprooting from before 1914 until now.

With respect to the question of "who and where from are we?" we need to dig into the storehouses of knowledge left by others be it our own people or non-Assyrian writers.

Based on the evidence from these sources, we are Assyrians, from the same bloodline as the mighty Assyrians who ruled over a vast territory in the Middle East for many years before Christ.

We are descendants of Shem, the father of Ashur (Name of the son of Noah. Genesis 10). As it is well-known, Ashur was the name of our first capital city, and also the name of the first king, known as god Ashur. Ashur had four brothers. One of them was named Arpakhshar. 300 years, or eight generations after Ashur, from the line of Arpakhshar, descended Abraham (Genesis 11). Abraham became the father of Israelites through his son Isaac. But Abraham had a second son Ishmael, born to his concubine Hagar. Ishmael is the father of Arabs.

But spiritually, all believers are known as the sons of Abraham. That is why we refer to him as "Baba Awraham".

Assyrians were ruled by famous kings for thousands of years. Kings such as Shalmanisar, Tiglath Pileser, Sargon, Sennacherib, Esarhaddon, Ashurbanipal, etc. In their height of power, the Assyrian kings conquered many countries, defeated many armies, performed great deeds, and brought civilization to many nations. But this great empire came to an end in 612 B.C. Not only many kingdoms such as the Babylonians, the Medians, Chaldeans, and others attacked its capital city Nineveh, but also natural disasters added to its sorrowful demise. The rainy storms and the melting of thick sheets of snow from the mountains caused the Tigris River to overflow its banks and great floods broke down the thick and high walls of the capital city. The enemy was then able to enter the city easily. The result was the downfall of the empire.

Thus the prophet Nahum's prophesy in 713 B.C. found in the first chapter of his book came true. So did Zephaniah's prophesy in 630 B.C. (See chapter two of Zephaniah.)

After the fall of Nineveh, the Assyrians established a small kingdom under the protection of Rome which was the world's greatest empire at that time. That kingdom survived for many years. Its capital was in Edessa now called Urfa which is in Turkey. That kingdom lasted until 336 A.D., at which time there was a war between Romans and Persians and Rome was defeated. Edessa fell into the hands of Persians, and the Assyrian kingdom came to an end. The Assyrians became dispersed in Urhai, Nisibis, Mosul, and Antioch. But the majority took refuge in the mountains of Kurdistan and dispersed till Van. From there some descended towards the plains of Urmia, Salamas, and Sulduz in Azerbaijan.

Starting from that time, Assyrians have lived in Azerbaijan for 1700 years. Some are still living there. Even though they have been subjected to persecution and pillage, they are still attached to their roots in that place.

## As to the name of our nation:

As far as I remember, and I am sure other old-timers will attest, until the start of World War I, we who lived in our ancient homeland called ourselves "Surayi". The Muslim inhabitants of Urmia and other towns in Azerbaijan called us "Asuri Millat" [Asuri Nation]. At other times they referred to us as Nasrani Millet (The Nazarite Nation), meaning the followers of Jesus the Nazarite. We were protected and esteemed in Muslim countries. There was a saying among our forefathers that before 1900 whenever a Christian was summoned in the court as a witness, the judge would not require him to swear an oath to the truth of his statements because the belief was the Nazarites do not lie. But there were others who called us "kafir" [infidel] because we were not believers in Islam.

At the start of World War I some of our brothers from Armenia joined us. The most famous was Dr. Freidoun Atouraya. I remember him well. Together with Benyamin Arsanis of Digala and other of their friends, they began to spread the name "Atouraya" for the first time among our people. This name appeared foreign and did not sit well with the people at the beginning. But slowly it took root and is

27

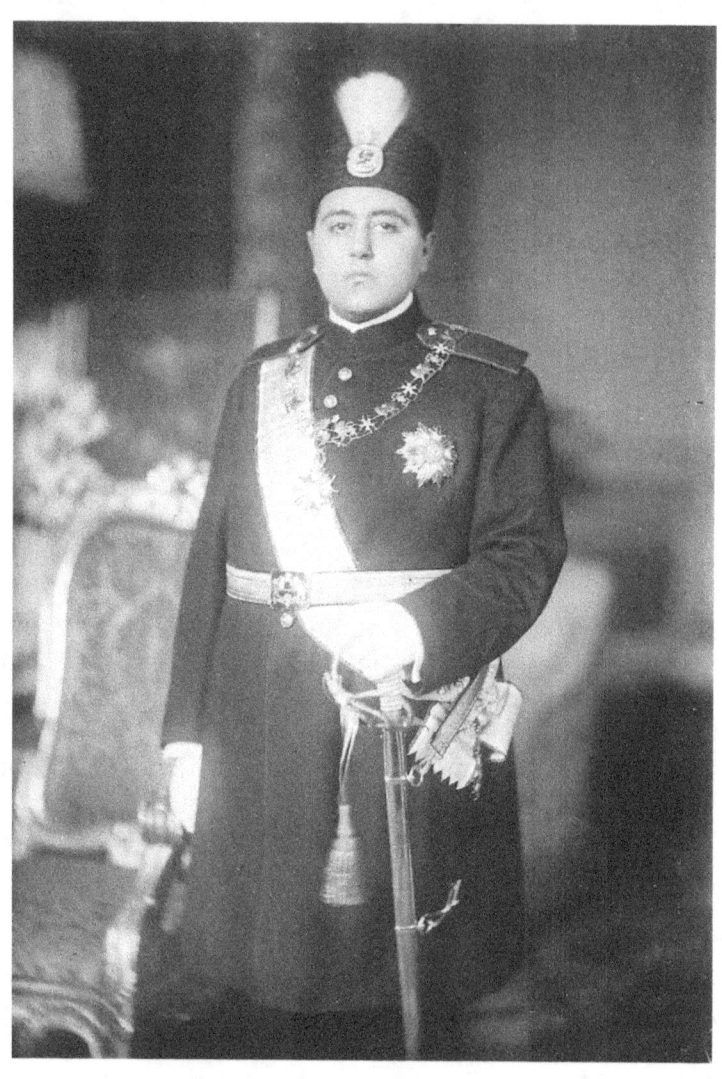

King Ahmad Shah while hospitalized in France, Reza Shah
gained power and replaced him.

accepted today. Understandably, replacing the name "Atouraya" with "Asuraya" is not difficult. In Some Assyrian dialects, the initial sound "A" is silent and the sound "t" is replaced by the sound "s". Why this change in name? I do not have a satisfactory answer.

In my estimation, although I am not sure if people will agree with me, the reason is that ancient Assyrians had acquired a reputation for being cruel rulers of vanquished nations especially of their treatment of war captives. After the fall of the empire, the Assyrians were dispersed among different nations and became a minority group. When they converted to Christianity and adhered to the motto "if slapped on the right cheek, offer the other", they attempted to bring a slight change in their national name so that in time the name "Atour" would be forgotten and the hatred towards that nation would fade away, and they would be known as "Surayi" instead.

Dr. Peera Sarmas in his book "Who Are We?" quotes Mar Toma Audo the Metropolitan of Urmia and Salamas, as follows: "The reference to the name "The Eastern Suryetta[1] Nation" is the nation that lived east of the River Euphrates, Atouraye [Assyrians]. They took on this name because the apostles were from the country of "Surya" [Syria], so they were called "Surayi".

The same author writes elsewhere "Because the apostles were all from "Surya" [Syria], and because our forefathers, the first Christians, had accepted Christianity wholeheartedly, and adhered to it earnestly, they preferred to be called after the name of the apostles. Therefore they abandoned their national name Assyrian and adopted the name Surayi,

---

[1]     Translator's Note: "Suryetta" is the feminine of "Suraya". The plural is "Surayi".

meaning Christians.

It is possible that the explanation of the above-mentioned authored is quite correct. But why is it that when we write our name, we add an initial silent "A" but when we write the name "Syria", we do not place the initial silent "A" in front of the name?

In Iraq, we were called "Ashuriyoun" the sound "t" being replaced by "sh".

Nonetheless, there is no doubt that we are Assyrians from the same bloodline as the ancient Assyrians even though, due to historical reasons, some of us are of mixed Jewish, Persian, and even Greek ancestry.

# Chapter 2
## The Assyrians Adopt Christianity

It is important to mention that the Assyrians adopted Christianity in the hands of some apostles a few years after the resurrection of the ascension of Jesus Christ.

The first apostle was Thomas. He was the apostle for the Assyrians until 45 A.D. Then he left for Malabar, India to preach the gospel and establish a Church in that country. Then Peter, sometimes called Shimun [Simon], took his place. He established a Church in Babel [Babylon] as noted in 1 Peter 14:5. After Peter left for Rome, then Addai (Thaddeus), one of the 70's, replaced him. This was the apostle whom Jesus sent to King Abgar 5th Ukama bar Shino, to cure his illness. According to historical documents, Thaddeus arrived in Abgar's court in 31 A.D., at the time when Tiberius was the governor of Rome in Jerusalem. So when Assyrians ruled Urhai, Jesus was in Israel. King Abgar invited Christ for a visit by sending three of his envoys: Marhad, Shamin Hagran, and Hannan. Their mission was to ask Jesus to cure the ailing king and also be a partner in ruling his small kingdom. Of course, Jesus had not come to be an earthly king. So Jesus did not go but sent his apostle Thaddeus to cure the king. The apostle was welcomed with great honors at the court. As soon as he arrived, he cured the king and many others who came to him. For this reason, many believed in Christianity and confessed their faith in one God in three Persons: Father, Son, and the Holy Ghost. They were then baptized in the name of Christ. Thus Christianity gradually spread among all the Assyrians.

After Christianity acquired a firm foothold among the Assyrians, then our forefathers took Christianity to the far corners of Asia such as China, Mongolia, India, and elsewhere.

As mentioned before, the first apostle among the Assyrians was Thomas. Tradition states that Thomas crossed the Lake of Urmia by walking on the water as one walks on dry land. For this reason, the Assyrians commemorate the third of Tamuz (July) of the Eastern Calendar and call it "Shilkha-d-Yamati"[2]. From then on people begin to swim in the Lake of Urmia.

With the advent of Mohammad, Islam became a strong religious force in the mountains and the plains where the Assyrians were dispersed after the fall of their kingdom in Urhai. Some of the inhabitants of these regions were forcefully converted to Islam by the sword. There came a time when the Muslims formed the majority of the population, and became the ruling power in the area. The Assyrians who lived in the mountains of Hakkari came under the rule of the Kurdish tribal overlords, and those who lived in the plains of Urmia, Salamas, and Sulduz became subjects of the Persian rulers.

Accordingly, these two nations Christians and Muslims, with different religious beliefs lived for many years harmoniously as neighbors and friends honoring the rights of one another.

---

[2]    It is an initiation feast at which time people swarm onto the shore to swim in the lake.

# Chapter 3
## An Introduction to Urmia

Urmia is the second town in rank compared to Tabriz in the province in Azerbaijan. It is located in the northern part of Iran. Its western neighbors are Salamas and Khoi situated close to Russian Azerbaijan. On the west, it flanks the mountains that separate Iran from Turkey. On the East, it borders the Lake of Urmia. The length of the Lake in some parts is 30 miles in others it is 35-40 miles.

Its name derives from the Assyrian language. Uri-d-Miya in Assyrian means the cradle of water. That is because it has abundant water to irrigate its fields and orchards.

Three rivers run through it. They have their source in the snowy mountains of Kurdistan and flow down into the Lake of Urmia. The first river is called Nazlu Chai and flows north of the town of Urmia. The second is centrally located and is called the Shahar Chai [The Town River]. The third is the Baranduz River in the south of the town.

These three rivers have made the plain of Urmia a veritable green paradise for both visitors and the inhabitants. The town is surrounded by vineyards, orchards of fruits of different kinds, and beautiful farmland adorned in natural beauty.

The town has splendid buildings. Around it are found villages with pastoral charm. Most villages are inhabited by Christians. Each village has a Church. The larger villages have 3-4 denominational Churches. There are also elementary schools in each village.

Some villages have a mixed Muslim-Christian population. But their dwellings are far from one another.

The town is enclosed with thick walls built with mud bricks that date back to ancient times. The length of these walls surrounding the town is 6.5 miles. Behind the walls are trenches. They are dry now but used to be filled with water to inhibit the enemy from reaching the walls.

The walls have 7 gates built with thick hardwood. The gates are dotted with spikes to make the gates sturdy. These gates were shut closed when the town was in danger of an enemy attack. In the gates were smaller doors to let one person enter the town when the larger gates were closed.

The inhabitants of Urmia are mostly Muslim of shiite denomination and of Turkish-speaking Afshar ancestry.

The Assyrian Christians form a minority in the region. It is estimated that before 1914 there were no more than 70,000 Assyrians in the region of Urmia and 30,000 in Salamas and Sulduz. There were a few thousand Armenians as well. A priest by the name of Yonan Shabaz gives an estimate of all Assyrians in Turkey and Iran before 1914 as follows:

13,000 Presbyterians, 60,000 Orthodox, and 200,000 Nestorians. He adds that in 1845 there was a great massacre of Assyrians in the Hakkari Mountains.[3] We also know that in 1880 the Kurdish Sheikh Obeidallah Suleiman led his tribe to sack Assyrian villages in Urmia. He even tried to destroy the town. But Dr. Cochran and the American missionaries

---

[3]     Translator's Note: The reference is to the Massacre of Assyrians by the Kurdish chief Badir-Khan.

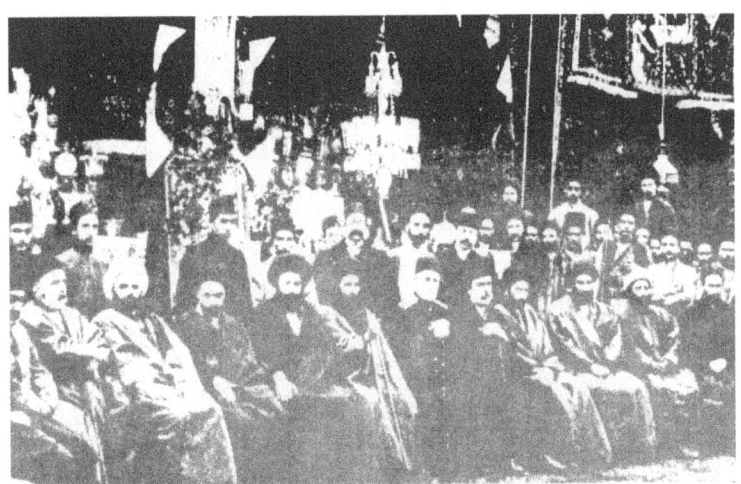

Top Picture: The Mullahs and the Mujtahidins together with the government leaders of Iran celebrate the ratification of the Constitution of Iran in Urmia, Circa 1908.

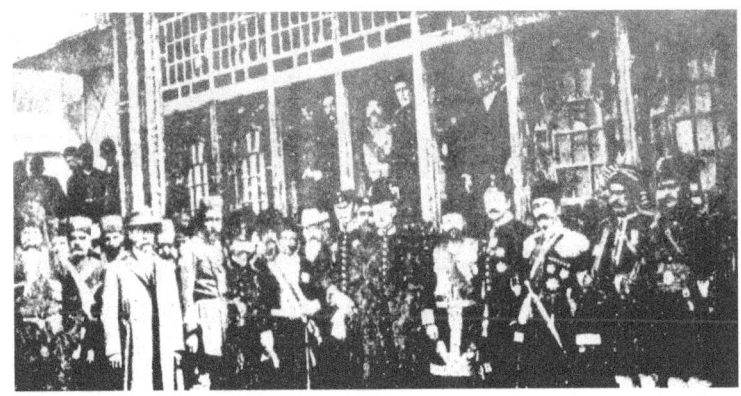

Bottom Picture: The government leaders together with foreign government dignitaries in the birthday celebration of Mohammad Ali Shah, the king of Iran in May 1908.

intervened and saved the town. this is because for many years the Kurdish leaders were cured of their ailments by the American Missionaries.

The original inhabitants of Urmia were generally of Zoroastrian faith (Fire Worshipers). In some villages are found high ash mounds from ancient times. Day and night fire-worshipers kept the fire burning. Our village Digala has a large ash mound which was the location for sacrificial offerings. There is also one in the village of Geogtapa, another in between the villages of Tarmani and Chargooshi, and in other villages as well.

But with the advent of Islam, many Zoroastrians were forcibly converted to Islam. But some escaped and fled to Bombay of India.

The climate of Urmia is evenly seasonal. There are four seasons: Spring, summer, fall, and winter. During springtime, most people begin to work in the fields. Owners of vineyards and orchards hire Muslim laborers to prune the fruit trees and vineyards and clean the debris from the vineyards and orchards. Dried-up branches and vine stems are collected and stored for winter fuel. In the fall, the fields are plowed and prepared to sow grain seeds. But the vegetable and herb gardens are planted in springtime to grow watermelons, melons, squash, and other kinds of vegetables and herbs.

Generally, Easter falls in the month of March. After religious services, people exchange good wishes on the occasion of the resurrection of Christ. After that day, for a whole week, the villagers spend their time in the orchards or the pastures. They play games or have colored egg contests as well as other amusements. Most families have on their dinner table

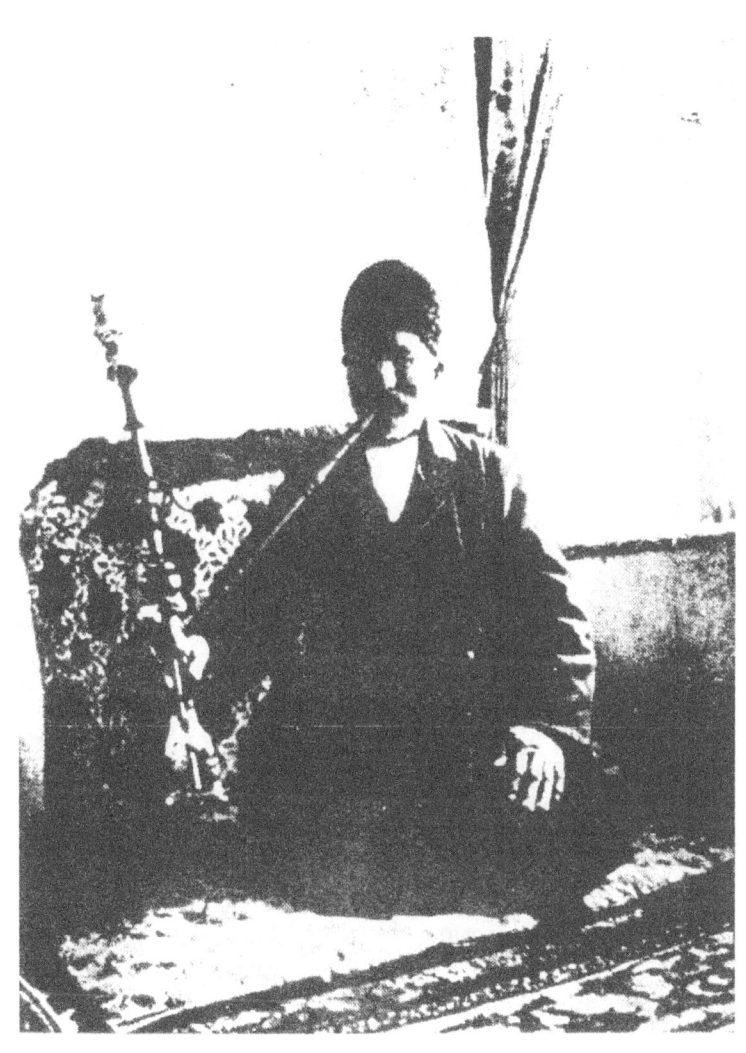

Kasha Babuna with his qalyon (Hookah).

the traditional Hareesa[4] among other dishes.

After spring, Urmia enters into a pleasant summer season.

It is very pleasant to sleep on the rooftop of cottages in the fresh air at night. It heals and strengthens the body. Spending the day in the orchards and fields in the summertime is very enjoyable. Most villagers leave their regular dwellings and move out to their vineyards for two and half months or half of the summer. There they live in cottages or small sheds. When the grapes are ripe, they begin first to lay the grapes down on the prepared ground [varazan] to dry as raisins for home consumption during winter months. Then they prepare sultana raisins and store them in their houses to be sold to local merchants. In their turn, the merchants export them to Russia or Germany. After that, the villagers select grapes to be hung from the ceiling of their basements for winter consumption. Some grapes are turned into wine. Then they collect the leftover grapes in the vineyard, crush them to extract the juice, and boil the juice to make molasses.

They shake loose the walnuts from the trees and store them away. They also pick and store other products such as watermelons, melons, quince, etc.

They make a variety of jams such as quince cooked in grape molasses, Halwa inserted with walnuts, etc. At the end of the summer, the storerooms in the houses overflow with products that the Lord has granted for the enjoyment of human beings.

---

[4]     Translator's Note: This dish is made with rooster or chicken meat boiled over low heat with wheat kernels overnight. It is then whipped into a mush and garnished with toasted coriander seed and melted butter.

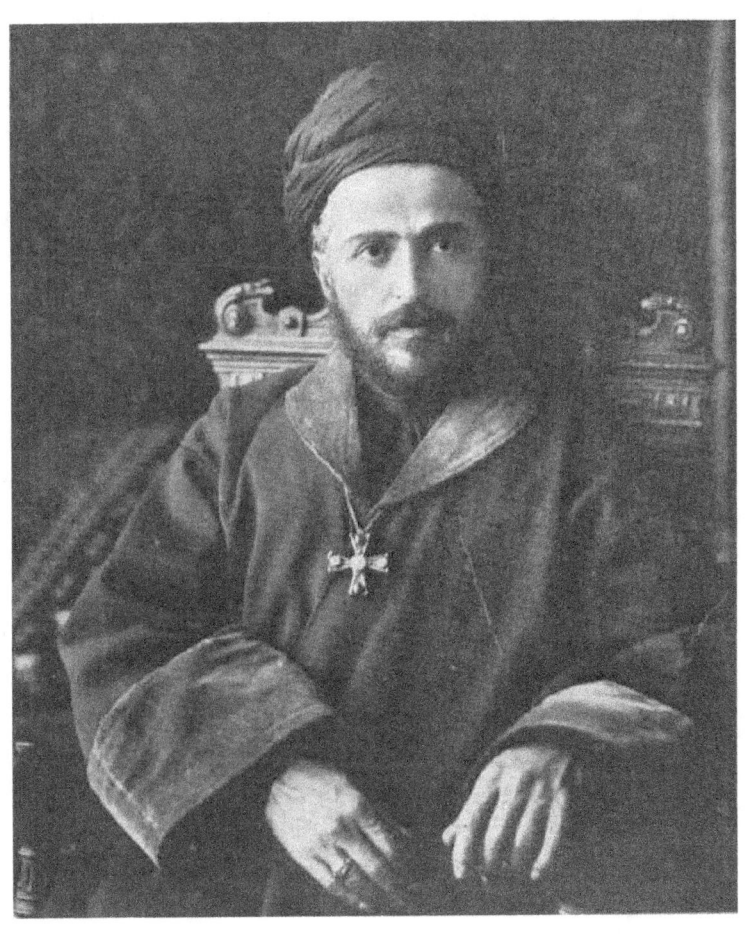

The Late Patriarch Mar Benyamin when invited by the Vali for a meeting in Van.

During the fall season, people get busy with arranging and organizing the storage of the summer produce. Wheat is ground into flour to last for the whole year. The floors of the rooms are swept and carpeted with beautiful Persian rugs in preparation for the cold months of the winter that last 3-4 months. During winter there is nothing to do except eat, drink, and visit relatives and friends. Some find small jobs to keep busy during winter. The majority of Assyrian villages are close to the town of Urmia. So some work in the town making boxes according to the sizes given to them. The boxes are used to pack sultana raisins for export.

At one time the central government was too weak to administer adequately the cities that were far from the capital of Tehran like Urmia and other towns in the province of Azerbaijan. Especially the social and legal needs of small minorities like the Assyrians and the Armenians were neglected. Due to the efforts of the American Mission, finally, each minority group was given the right to establish its own civic association to settle internal disputes. Furthermore, all Christians excepting the Catholics who abstained from participation were given the right to form an interdenominational council. This council had the power to decide and impose its resolutions upon the Christians as well as administer justice in fairness without bias or favoritism. In effect, the council functioned as a parliament in a regular country.

# Chapter 4

## The Condition of the Christians on the Eve of World War I (1914-1918)

At the end of the second chapter, I referred to the amicable relations and goodwill that existed between the Christians and the Muslims. But there came a time especially in the Kurdistan mountains when the Kurdish emirs (tribal leaders) vied for power against one another and war broke out among them. In these power struggles the Assyrians were caught in the middle. They had to take sides and support the emir whose subjects they were. On such occasions, the Assyrians suffered greatly. Not only their farms remained unattended, but also their flocks were stolen. Worse yet, some of their fighting men were killed.

Taking sides created hatred towards all the Assyrians in Kurdistan and led to vengeful fanatical religious reprisals against them. The previous neighborly relations and loyalties were forgotten.

A case in point is the horrific massacre of Assyrians in 1843 by the joint forces of Bader Khan the emir of Bohtan, Nurallah the emir of Julmarik, and Zeinolbeg, the emir of the Lower Tkhuma.

With the intervention of the British, the Turkish government punished these Kurdish emirs [tribal leaders]. They were

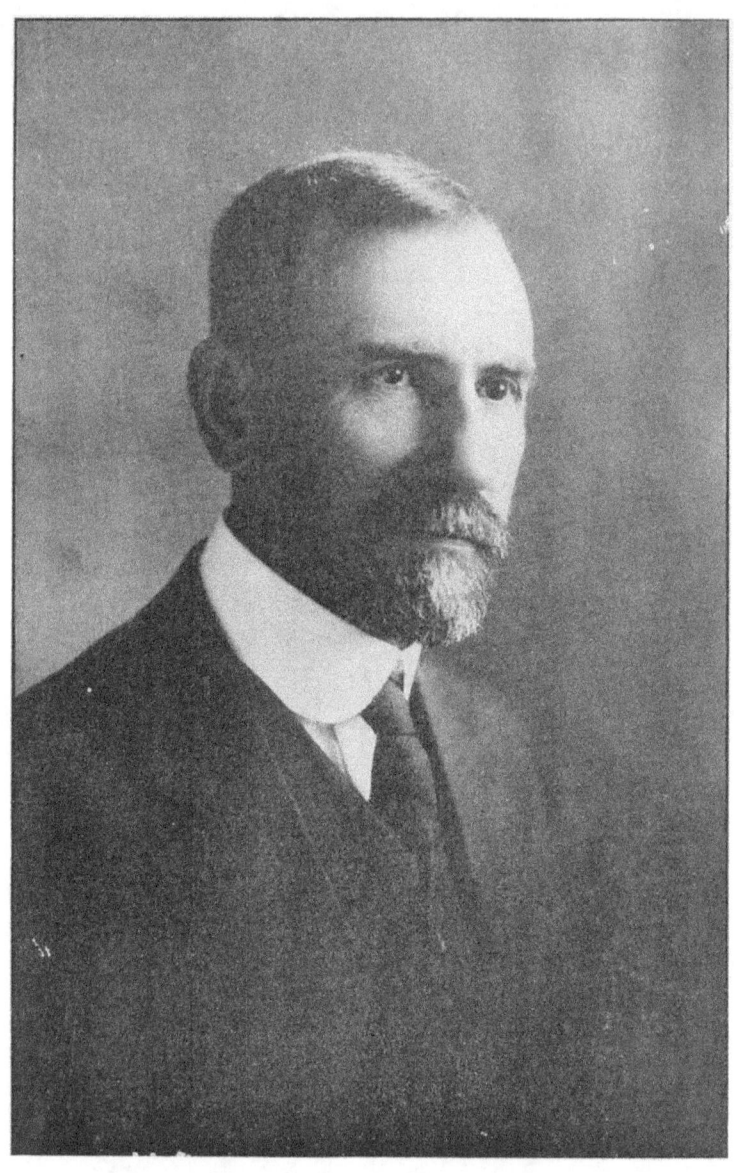

Dr. William Ambrose Shedd, Head of the American Presbyterian Mission in Iran.

exiled to the island of Crete in the Mediterranean Sea. To a large extent, calm was restored in Kurdistan. The displaced Assyrians were returned back to their villages. Their lands which were confiscated by these emirs were returned back to them.

## The Meeting between Patriarch Mar Benyamin and the Turkish Vali (governor):

As the prospects of World War I whetted the appetite of the Turkish leaders, on August 3, 1941, Tahsin Pasha, the Vali [governor] of Van invited the Patriarch Mar Benyamin to a meeting in the city of Van.

The Patriarch arrived in Van as scheduled. At this meeting, the vali gave assurances that the Assyrians would be protected on the condition that they remain neutral and do not side with the Russians since Turkey was entering the war against the Russians and the Allied Forces. The Patriarch agreed and when he returned to Kurdistan, he sent messages to all the Assyrian tribal leaders to maintain neutrality and stay loyal to the central government in Turkey.

But two months after that, in October 1914, about fifty Christians from the village of Gawar were arrested on false pretenses and taken to Turkey where they were executed. These executions took place elsewhere in Kurdistan as well. Moreover, a number of Assyrian villages were pillaged, men and women abducted, and young girls were outraged by the cruel Turkish soldiers.

These events charted the destiny of the Christians in Turkey and were a sign of alarm to Christians in the Middle East on the eve of World War I in 1914. The animosity of Muslims towards Christians came crashing down on them. The result was a distress call from Christians everywhere they lived. The greatest catastrophe was that which occurred to our brothers the Armenians of Van and the surrounding villages where thousands were cruelly massacred by the Turks.

At this time Turkey officially entered the war on the side of Germany. Then Turkey spread propaganda in its newspapers and in other media of communication to the effect that Emperor Wilhelm of Germany strongly advocated the conversion of all inhabitants of Turkey to Islam. Of course, this was false news and had no basis in truth. Nevertheless, it was very encouraging to the Muslims and emboldened them. Religious hatred spread across the border to the Muslims of Urmia and Azerbaijan.

The most dangerous event for the Christians at this time was the retreat of the Russian forces from Urmia and the surrounding villages to the Caucasus under General Chornazobof in December 1914 of the Western calendar. This was to strengthen the defense line against Turkey which had amassed a large army in Sari Kamesh with the intent to take the Caucasus while Russia was busy fighting the Germans on another front. By moving its military forces to the Caucasus, Russia intended to prevent the Turkish takeover of the area. The retreat of the Russian forces alarmed the Christians in Southern Russia as well as in the villages near the border of Turkey. The inhabitants fled to the interior of the Caucasus for safety as they feared that Turkey might occupy southern Russia and take the inhabitants captive.

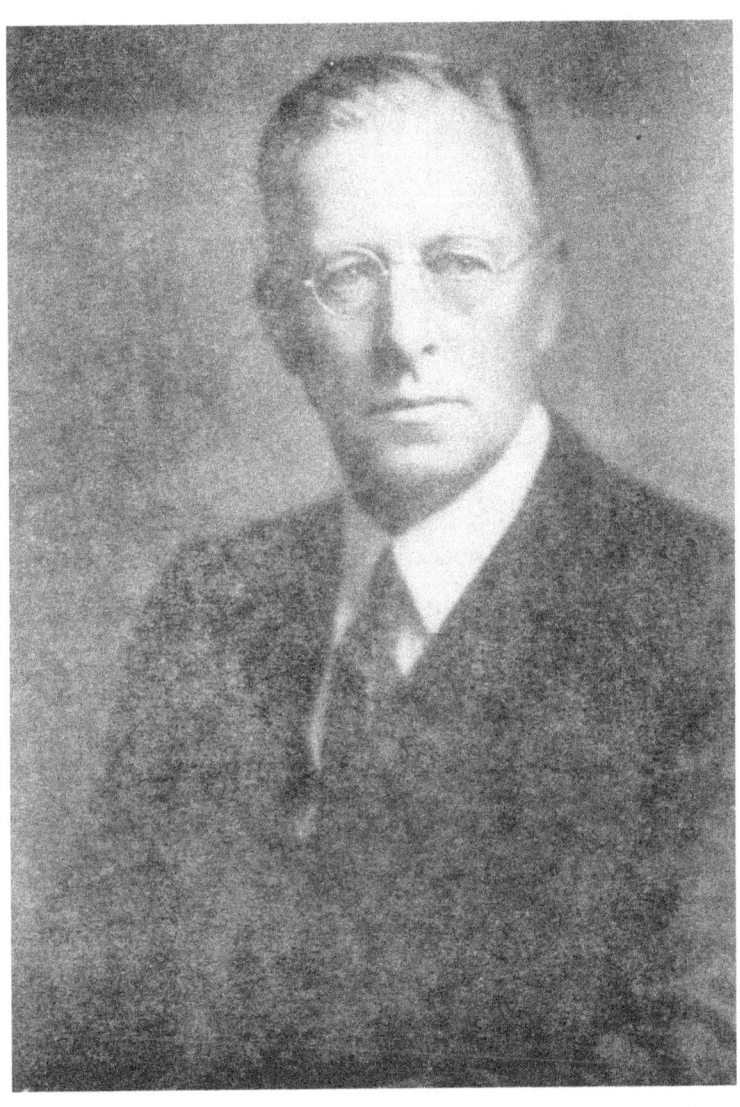

Dr. Ike P. Packard the Physician at the American Presbyterian Mission Hospital in Urmia

## The Departure of the Russian Forces from Urmia and The flight of some Christians into the American Presbyterian Mission compound and others into the French Catholic Mission:

After the retreat of the Russian forces from Urmia and the surrounding villages, the Turks [Ottoman Turks] and the Kurds took the opportunity to descend upon the Plain of Urmia and began to pillage the Christian villages, and kill the people, young and old, indiscriminately.[5]

Terrified, the Christians hastily abandoned their villages and sought refuge for their families and themselves in the American Mission yard in the town of Urmia. Others ran to the French Mission in the village of Golpatalikhan. A few were given protection in the homes of their local Turkish friends.

About 10,000 Assyrians who were from the North of Urmia that is, from the villages around the Nazlu River, fled behind the retreating Russian forces into Russia. To these were added people around the highlands of Margawar, Targawar, Salamas, and elsewhere. The number reached up to 30,000 refugees. This was in the middle of winter, on icy roads. But they thought it was better to leave than stay in their villages in fear of the impending massacre.

Some of these refugees died on the icy roads; others perished from disease and hunger. But a large number reached Tiflis in

---

[5]    Translator's Note: The author uses the term "Turk" to refer to the Ottoman Turks in the country of Turkey. He uses the term "Afshars" to refer to the Iranian Turks native to the Province of Azerbaijan in Northwest Iran.

46

the Caucasus. Some returned back to their homes when the Russian army reentered Urmia. But others stayed and became dispersed in the villages of that country.

It is important to mention at this point that the United States of America had not entered the war at that time. Nevertheless, Dr. William Ambrose Shedd who was the head of the Evangelical Mission in Urmia raised the American flag over the Mission gate as a declaration that the Christian refugees at the mission were under the protection of the United States of America. The Turks were greatly annoyed by this gesture since Dr. Shedd was not an appointed American consul or an American government representative. But the town leaders and other government officials supported Dr. Shedd's action which was to protect the Iranian Christians from the hands of the Turks and Kurds both of whom were foreign occupiers in the Iranian territory. So, the Turks unwillingly tolerated and respected the authority of the American flag. The same was true when the French Mission raised the French flag upon its mission compound.

Thousands of fugitives from Targawar, Margawar, and Baranduz district poured into the mission grounds to escape certain massacres.

In 1918 Dr. Shedd was officially appointed as the American vice-consul and was recognized by other governments as such.

Several times Dr. Shedd contacted the local government officials and asked them to set in place a police station for the protection of town people and for maintaining law and order in the area. But he was not successful. The real reason was disunity among the government officials. A new political faction had come into existence that wanted to remove the Persian Shah and establish a constitutional monarchy instead. Thus the local Christians remained at the mercy of the Turkish and Kurdish occupiers who thirsted for their blood.

At this time Tabriz was in the grips of similar mayhem with the difference that there the Americans had an official U.S. Consulate. Mr. Gordon Paddock was the consul and he took the Assyrians and the Armenians that lived in Tabriz under the protection of the American flag. There were other nationals that needed protection as well such as the British, French, Italians, Russians and Australian citizens.

## A Great Deliverance:
## The Intervention of Dr. Ike P. Packard to deliver thousands of the inhabitants of Geogtapa from an impending massacre.

A great deliverance had been planned for the village of Geogtapa. This is a village five miles to the East of the town of Urmia.

In that large village, there were fugitives from other adjacent villages who had taken shelter there when the Kurds were looting their villages. A horde of Kurds had swarmed into Geogtapa. They were not only looting, but also killing whoever they came across. The village people had locked themselves inside the village Church in order to protect their families and themselves. The Kurds had encircled the Church thirsty for Assyrian blood. The Kurds were attacking and the men inside were counter-attacking with primitive weapons no more than 14 crude rifles. At this critical time, by God's providence, the alarm cry reached the American Mission Compound in town. Dr. Packard was the chief physician of the hospital called Qala-d-Sahabi located in a large tract of land (about 12 acres), one and three fourth miles north of town. He quickly sent a letter by Haydar Ali, a loyal Iranian, to Kanini Agha the chief of a large Kurdish tribe who had just arrived in Urmia with his entourage. Dr. Packard had cured many Kurdish chiefs and their families from various diseases at that hospital and was highly esteemed by Kurds. Kanini Agha was a close friend of Dr. Packard. In the letter, Dr. Packard asked Kanini Agha to intervene and save the beleaguered Christians of Geogtapa.

Immediately Kanini Agha, together with a few other Kurdish chiefs, mounted their horses at 9:00 o'clock at night and took Dr. Packard with them and headed to Geogtapa carrying the American flag with them. They stopped the Kurdish siege on the Church and released the captives on the condition that the men surrender their weapons to the Kurds.[6]

The Christian captives, women, and children of all ages, were taken to the American Mission compound the same night. But Geogtapa as well as the adjacent villages with all their belongings remained in the possession of the Kurdish marauders.

---

[6]     Translator's Note: : Another person who was present in the group of rescuers was an Assyrian physician by the name of Dr. David S. Daniel (Father of the famous composer William Daniel) who was loved and esteemed by the Kurds as he had cured many of their family members.

As mentioned earlier, after the retreat of the Russian forces, we, the Assyrians, fled from our villages and took shelter in the American and French Mission Compound. The mission grounds were not big enough to accommodate 15-20 thousand refugees. So the missionaries rented 5 adjacent houses and opened entryways between them to accommodate as many of these refugees as possible. In addition, there were other safe houses for refugees such as Sardari[7], the Episcopalian Mission compound, and the Orthodox Church. All these buildings were under the protection of the American flag and they were full of Christian fugitives who had fled their villages.

All that winter until the spring of 1915 that is, for 5 months the fugitives stayed in these compounds. 15-20 thousand individuals were sustained daily with 6 tons of bread which were bought from the town Muslims and carried on the backs of porters. This arrangement was made by the mayor of the town of Urmia. But later we found out that the flour was mixed with chalk. People became sick and 20-30 people died every day.

On March 11 , 1915 shortly before we were released from confinement, a large contingent of Turks arrived in Urmia numbering from 15-20 thousand soldiers under Khalil Beg. Khalil Beg was the uncle of Anwar Pasha. He was second in command to Rashid Beg the General of the Turkish army in Azerbaijan. This new battalion arrived from Sulduz and

---

[7]     Sardari was the mission college for the sons of wealthy Muslim nobility and rich Jewish students. Its purpose was to evangelize Muslims and Jews.

thereabouts. The purpose was to strengthen the Turkish forces around Khoi and Salamas against the Russians. They stayed in Urmia for a few days and then moved to Salamas. A few days after the arrival of the Turkish forces in Salamas, they came face to face with the Russian forces. Then a bloody battle ensued after which the defeated Turkish forces retreated towards Turkey on the 15th of May. Then Chornazobof, the General of the Russian army, sent a letter to Patriarch Mar Benyamin asking him to raise a force comparable to that of Khalil Beg to block his way. (This is when the Ashirat[8] tribes were still at their posts.)

At that time the Russians were in control of the borders extending from Julfa, Khoi, Salamas, Urmia, Sulduz, up to Savoch bolagh.

Before the Turks evacuated Salamas, the soldiers that were already there under Lieutenant Jodat Beg went to the Catholic Mission and seized 800 people. They were mostly Armenian men, women, and children. They massacred all of them. This atrocity happened when the Turks were fighting the Russians.

It needs to be mentioned that Lieutenant Jodat Beg was a graduate of the French Catholic College in Beirut.

When the victory of the Russians over the Turks became certain, on May 15, 1915, the Russian forces returned back to Urmia. We, the Christians, were set free and left the American

---

[8]     Translator's Note: The Ashirats were independent Assyrian Tribes in the mountains of Kurdistan nominally subject to the Ottoman Sultan.

Mission compound. Then the high-ranking Muslims took our place there because of the reprisals of Christians against those who had been the cause of looting and killings. The Muslim leaders were given protection and care in the American Mission compound for six months.

We returned to our ruined and empty homes because everything had been carried away. People were sick and dying. Many of these emaciated refugees died because not only their homes were empty of basic furnishings, but also because there was no seed to plant a crop. The American Missionaries helped by providing seed and some furnishings donated by the Near East Relief in Tabriz.

The number of dead reached 4000 during the time that the refugees were sheltered in the Mission Compounds. Many died after they were freed.

As mentioned before, when Dr. Shedd raised the American flag to safeguard the fugitives, a large number of Turks complied with the government's stand to respect the American flag. So they refrained from attempting to kill us. But every now and then the Turkish officials came in and apprehended a distinguished person and incarcerated him. Then they demanded a ransom for his release. Otherwise, the person would be killed.

The first time this occurred was on March 6, 1915. The Turkish soldiers under Badri Afandi came and arrested Mar Elia, the bishop of the Orthodox Church. When Dr. Shedd heard this, he immediately asked the Iranian government officials to intervene because Mar Elia was a respected and humble person and had many friends and followers. The Iranian leaders and the Muslim elders together with Dr. Shedd tried hard to save this man's life. With these attempts, Mar Elia was finally set free after 20 days, on March 29. He was ransomed for 5,000.00 Tumans equivalent to $150,000 today. Later on, Dr. Eskhaq Daniel titled Hakim Logman was taken as he was making the round of patients in the Mission hospital. He too was released with the efforts of the missionaries and government officials. He had many Muslim friends. Actually, the title "Logman" was awarded to him by the officials of the Iranian government for his excellence as a physician. His ransom was paid with Mission funds.

Five more times the Turks repeated this barbarous act that is, the incarceration of prominent people for purposes of filling their pockets with money. They apprehended Rev. Nestorus Malik and Professor Yohanan Mar Nukha. Shamasha (Deacon) Lazar was arrested in the street by the servant of Shahbandar (The Turkish Consul) and was taken to the

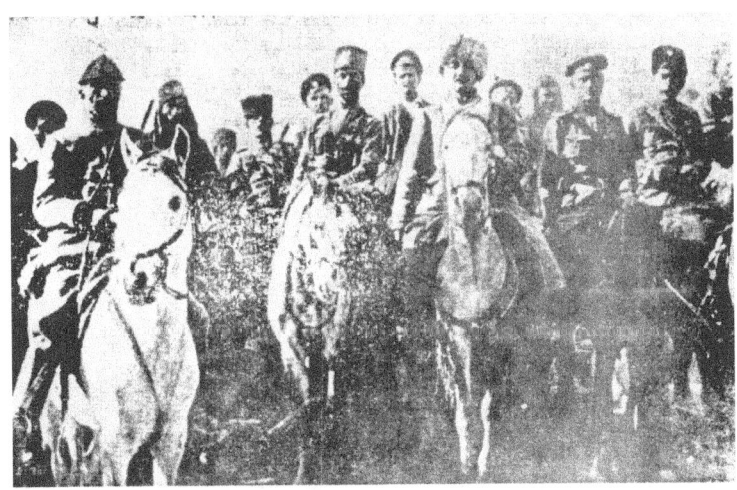

Agah Petros with the Officers in Charge of Canons.

53

consulate. Deacon Bahra was apprehended at the French Catholic Mission. Rabi (title for a teacher) David of Digala was arrested elsewhere.

Eventually, the Mission funds were depleted. Mr. Hugo Miller tried to borrow money with interest elsewhere to buy back these captives held by the Turks. The Assyrian brides gave all their jewelry to be pawned for a loan to purchase these captives back.

One time when these hijackers were parading in front of the Mission entrance, suddenly they found an occasion to enter through the gate. The weary and terrified people inside began to run to the interior of the compound. Finally, Mr. Miller who always carried a cane came to the gate and with the help of Iranian police, and another local Turk (Afshar) succeeded in wisely and politely steering the intruders out of the compound.

When we took shelter in the American Mission compound, the inhabitants of Gulpashan, a village located 6 miles to the east of Urmia, stayed in their homes because the Turkish Consul had assured them safety from Kurdish or the Muslims of Urmia. Rajib Beg (The Turkish Consul) sent a contingent of Turkish soldiers to protect the village. These soldiers were being paid by the inhabitants of Gulpashan. This arrangement worked for a couple of months. The soldiers were paid regularly and on time. But these predator soldiers began to pry on the inhabitants. There were a few Christian families from other villages that had taken shelter in Gulpashan. They were targeted as well. At one time 73 men were taken, tied together, taken to the village cemetery, and brutally murdered. Three wounded men had fallen under

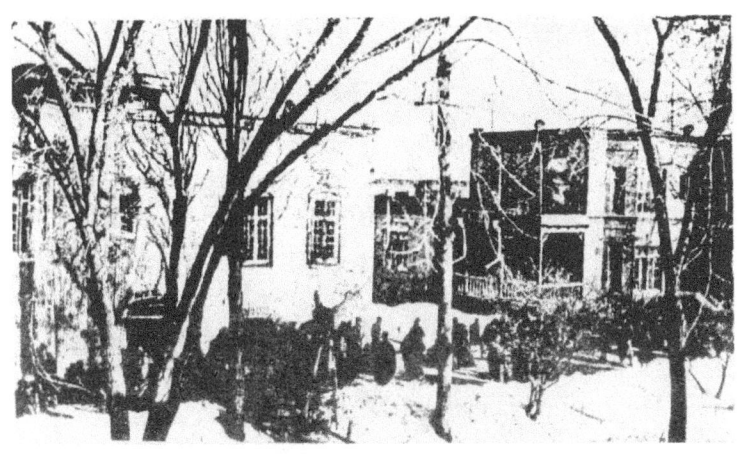

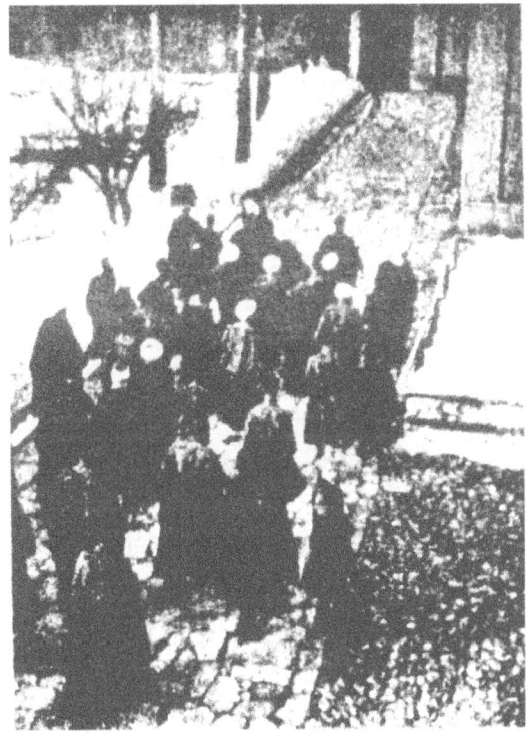

Both pictures depict the Mullahs and the Mujtahidins in the yard of the American Presbyterian Mission submitting the town to the charge of Dr. Shedd after the fall of Urmia by the hands of Assyrians.

dead corpses and were still alive. At night they made their way to the American Mission compound.

After a few days, this barbarous act was repeated. The soldiers killed 50 men in the French Mission compound. They tied them together and took them to the Jewish Hill and murdered them there.[9] 60 other men were taken and used as porters to carry heavy loads from Gawar to Urmia.[10] After reaching Urmia, they were taken to Kalla of Ismael Agha and were shot in the valley below. Two of the wounded men Two of the wounded men escaped at night and reached the Mission yards.

Because of the crowded conditions, the Typhus epidemic broke out and spread among the refugees. The first person who died from it was Shamasha (deacon) Shmuel Khoshaba Millat Bashi [meaning head of a nation]. Rumor was that the Turks were planning to abduct him. As we were told, he became sick out of fear and passed away on May 8, 1915. The wife of Dr. McDowell died of Typhus as well. So did a teacher named Ms. Madeleine Froshet from Switzerland. She taught the children of the missionaries the French language. Ms. Lenorar Shobel, the Director of the Fiske Seminary for women, also died of this disease. This disease sent many to their graves.

From the villages, there was an outcry that women and girls were being abducted by Kurds and the Turks. The missionaries asked for assistance from the Iranian soldiers to find the whereabouts of the hostages and buy them back. One time an alarm sounded about many women and girls

---

[9]      There is a hill near the town of Urmia called the Jewish Hill. It is a Jewish cemetery.

[10]      Translator's Note:  Gawar , in Turkey, is 60 miles away from the Iranian border.

being abducted. Dr. Shedd, with the help of the town governor, Azeen–al-Soltaneh found up to 200 girls who were taken by Kurds and the Turks. They were able to rescue them with much difficulty and at a high price. They brought them to the Mission grounds. This Sardar (governor) who was the highest authority in town, tried to help in any way he could directly or by means of others even though he did not have much power in those cases. It was with the prompting of this Sardar that a famous Muslim who was the son of Haji Wakil, paid 500 Tumans to release these captives.

One time a Muslim lady, in conservative attire, brought a lot of bread on the back of a porter. She handed it over to Mr. Miller at the entrance gate of the American Mission and asked to distribute it to the needy as charity. Another time some merchants sent the meat of an ox to be distributed as charity to the Christian refugees. Another Muslim came forward and gave a promissory note to send 15 bags of wheat to the Christian refugees. Such occasional aid was given by some devout Muslims especially those who had been friends with the Christians.

Every now and then the Turks came to the missionaries and told them to send the refugees back to their villages claiming that they were not in danger. But the Christians were too afraid to leave.

Once Shahbandar, the Turkish Consul, invited some people to the consulate and asked them to voluntarily provide 50,000 shirts to the Turkish soldiers. The guests promised to prepare 10,000 only. This was to extract forced labor from the captive refugees.

## The Exodus of the Mountain Tribes to Azerbaijan:

A fierce fight rages between the Christian Ashirats [Independent Assyrian Mountaineers] on one side, and the Kurds and Turks on the other.

The Turks were well prepared and equipped with ammunition. After that violent encounter, our brothers, the Ashirats, could not resist the enemy. They left their homes and all their possessions and fled to Urmia, Salamas, and Khoi. But in the summer of 1916, with the help of some Russian Kazaks, they tried to fight their way back to their homes. But again the Turks, assisted by the Kurds, and with better arms and the larger number of fighters, held them back. So our Ashirat brothers returned to Azerbaijan defeated again.

The conflict between the Muslims and the Christians was on the increase because of religious fanaticism.

The retreat of the Russian contingent to the Caucasus and return back to Azerbaijan took place several times during the war. Each time that one side won, the other retreated.

## Patriarch Mar Benyamin Invited by the Uncle of the Russian Tsar:

In December of 1915, Patriarch Mar Benyamin was invited by Prince Nicolai, the uncle of the Russian Tsar, to a meeting in Tiflis. The patriarch was received with great honors. At the same time, Emperor Tsar sent the Patriarch a letter with promises that all necessary protection would be provided to Assyrians to ensure their safety at home.

When the patriarch returned back in September 1916, the Russian contingent was still present in Urmia and environs.

Upon the request of the Russians, another meeting was arranged between a Russian general and the Patriarch Mar

Benyamin. The purpose of this meeting was to organize two battalions from the Ashirats in order to support the Russian army in the war effort against the Turks. Thus two battalions were formed equipped with ammunition and trained by Russian officers. As we will see later, they became a mighty force in several bloody battles against our enemies the Turks and the Kurds.

## Bolsheviks in Russia:

A misfortune to our nation and the world as a whole: at a time when more than ever we needed the Russian forces in the war, unfortunately in October 1917 in the middle of World War I, there was a revolution in Russia and the Bolsheviks came to power. The royal family was executed. The Russian army withdrew completely from the Azerbaijan front except for a few officers and soldiers who stayed in Urmia. The reason for their stay was, first, they were not sympathetic to the Bolsheviks. Second, they were committed to helping us. Among them were three generals: Kuzmin, Semanof, and Kondratyev together with a large number of officers and infantrymen.

Some of these Russian foot soldiers were relieved of their duties officially and engaged in reprehensible behavior. They destroyed the arsenal and sold the weapons to Turks, Kurds, and the Assyrians indiscriminately. They also robbed the town bazaar and set fire to it. Finally, the Russian officers stopped them.

## An Important meeting between the Patriarch Mar Benyamin and General Semanoff of Russia:

In December of 1917 an important meeting takes place between Patriarch Mar Benyamin who came from Salamas, to meet General Semanoff in Urmia.

The main purpose of the meeting was to plan the war strategy. Present in the meeting were General Gozmin, the commander-in-chief of both Assyrian battalions, Captain Gracy, the official representative of the British military mission in the Russian Caucasus under the command of General Ophil Shor.

The main purpose of Captain Gracy's presence was to officially declare that the Assyrians were part of the Allied Forces and to urge them to continue to fight against the enemy so that at the end of the war they could obtain the rights of freedom (independence). Another person present in the meeting was the American Vice-Consul, a Red Cross representative, Dr. William A. Shedd, and Agha Petros.

Captain Gracy suggested that the Patriarch meet with Simko Ismail Agha Shikak to discuss plans to unite against the Turks. This is because Simko had promised the British to join the Allied Forces. Captain Gracy had met Simko on his way to the meeting at which time the latter had given him that promise.

## What is the Outward Appearance of a Turk?

An article in a London periodical printed during World War I describes the character of a Turk as follows:

1. The Turk as a master is without mercy.
2. As a representative of his government to negotiate agreements or discuss the terms of an agreement, he is a crafty Byzantine.
3. As a soldier he is a ferocious fighter like an animal.
4. As a conqueror, he has no conscience and is a brute.
5. Having accomplished his goal, he pretends to be humble and pitiful so that those who do not know him, cannot believe how cruel and heartless he is.

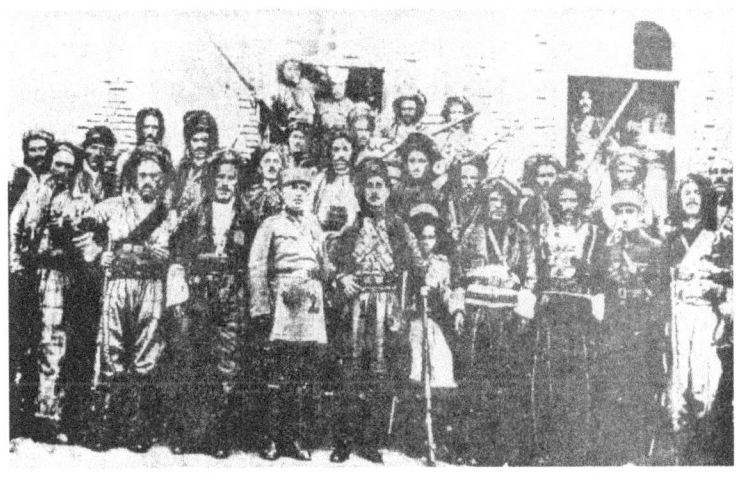

The Kurdish Leadership: (1) Ismail Agha; (2) [Chavish of the Iranians?] with a number of Kurdish chiefs from surrounding regions gathered for this memorable Kurdish day.

# Chapter 5

## The Condition of the Assyrians in Azerbaijan At the beginning of World War I

World War I is still ranging on. The animosity between Christians and Muslims has reached its zenith. The spirit of revenge even among the Afshars (local Turks) is gaining momentum. The leaders of our nation are negotiating with the Muslim leaders of Urmia in a futile effort to maintain peace at a time when both Assyrians and Muslims are armed and infuriated against one another.

On February 22, 1918 after the breakdown of peace talks, the Muslim inhabitants of Urmia under Ashrat Homayoon, the commander of the Persian Forces in Urmia that year, staged an attack on us from all sides of the town. During the two days of fierce fighting our artillery under the Russian officers in Digala and Charbash that is, on either side of the town, were firing at the enemy non-stop. In desperation, the Muslims lifted up a white flag as a sign of surrender from the rooftops and the windows of their houses. (They were some white sheets and fragments of white linen.)

At the end, the heaps of death on both sides were everywhere. A lot of Mullahs [Muslim priests] and Mujtahideen [high-ranking Muslim clergy] came to town to submit Urmia to Dr. Shedd. Now the government of the town fell into the hands of the Assyrians.

After the surrender of the Muslims, Ashrat Homayoon, the commander of the Muslim Forces, found sanctuary with Monseigneur Sontag, the French metropolitan representing Pope in the French Catholic Mission. Agha Petros, who was the commander of the Assyrian forces, asked Monseigneur Sontag to surrender Ashrat Homayoon as required by law, to be tried in a military court. But the Metropolitan refused to do so. Ashrat Homayoon and his family were under the protection of the French Mission for as long as we were ruling Urmia that is, until July 18, 1918 of the Eastern Calendar. On that day we fled Urmia.

It is noteworthy that six months after we had left Urmia and fled to Sayen Qala, Ashrat Homayoon murdered the French metropolitan instead of thanking him for protecting him and his family.

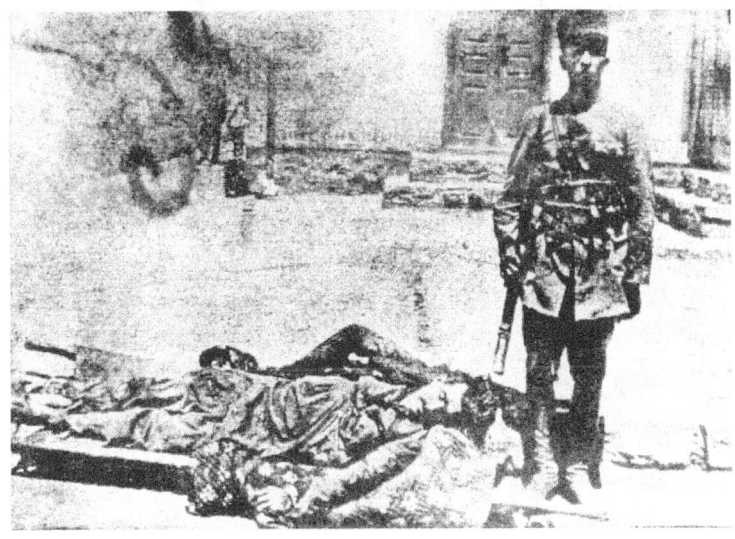

Simko (Ismail Agha) killed by the Iranians in the town of Ushnuq in 1930.

The same traitor gave orders to assassinate Mar Toma Audo, the Metropolitan of Urmia and Salamas, together with seven other priests at the French Mission, three Presbyterian Evangelist, as well as many others.

When Urmia fell into our hands, the Christians did not want to be the sole rulers of Urmia. They tried to organize a council composed of both Christians and Muslims to administer the affairs of the town. When the council was formed, the previous governor, Sardar Assim-al-Saltaneh was chosen instead of the crafty and treacherous Ashrat Homayoon.

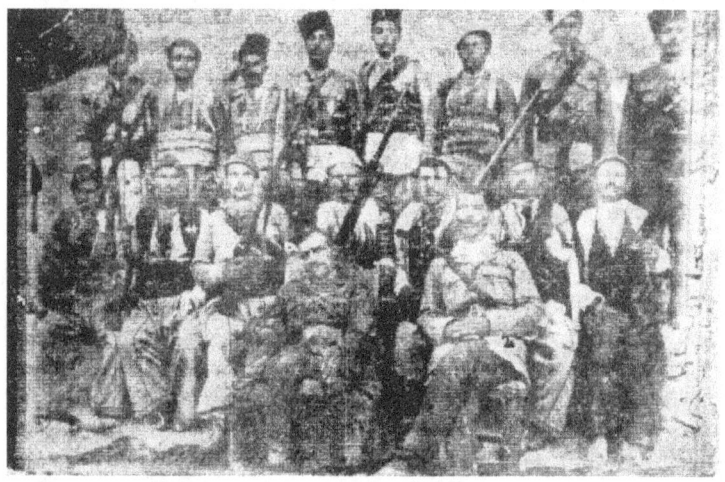

Malik Khoshaba Yossip with (1) his Tyari armed fighters and with Agha Mirza (2) The brother of Agha Petros

Sardar was more sympathetic to Assyrians. The courthouse of this man, upon the orders of Agha Petros, was protected by Assyrian guards to prevent the Assyrians and Armenians from hurting him. But one day there came a deacon from the village of Wazirabad and asked permission from the Assyrian guards to see the Sardar. He claimed that this Sardar was the landlord of the village and that he was his agent and the overseer of his lands. The guards believed Deacon Parhad, and let him in. After entering the courthouse, the guards heard sounds of gunfire. Deacon Parhad had murdered the Sardar as well as another Muslim clergy.

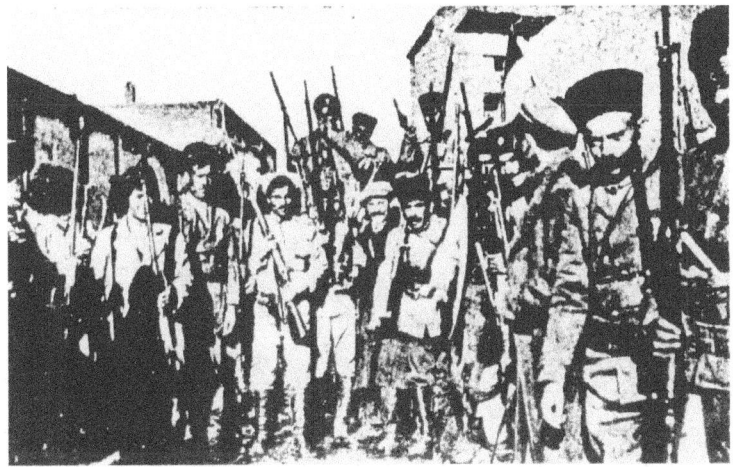

The Assyrian Armed Fighters after the fall of Urmia

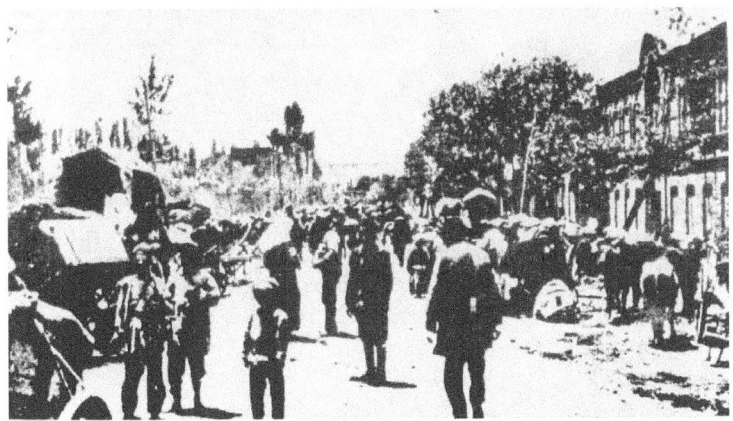

The Exodus of Assyrians and Armenians from Urmia to Sayen Qala

The guards arrested the culprit and brought him to Agha Petros for judgment. As a punishment, the deacon was hanged in front of the house of the Sardar.

In 1918, after our victory in Urmia, the Russian consul Basil Nikitine returns to Urmia again. At the same time a military mobile clinic of the French Catholic (Lazarists), under the supervision of Dr. Pauil Caujole, sailed to Urmia to help the sick.

## The Murder of Mar Benyamin by Simko Ismail Agha:

On March 3, 1918, a sad incident occurred in our nation. Patriarch Mar Benyamin was invited by Simko (Ismail Agha) to visit him for the purpose of forging an alliance and establishing friendship between the Assyrians and the Kurds.

The Patriarch with a small number of armed bodyguards went to meet Simko in Kohneh Shahr of Salamas.

The Patriarch with his dignitaries including Khoshaba Shmuel Khan, his brother Eshai, and four Russian bishops were received with high honors by Simko. They were escorted to their seats in the house. After an amicable give and take over tea, the meeting ended.

The Patriarch and his entourage got up to leave. Again they were escorted with much honor especially by the treacherous Simko who helped the Patriarch into his carriage and even kisses his hand.

As soon as Simko returned to his quarters, and the Patriarch was just seated in his carriage, a bullet was fired from a window at the Patriarch. This was a sign to avert those waiting in ambush. A lot of Kurds on rooftops began to bombard the Patriarch and company with bullets. Thus the Patriarch and 47 fighters together with the four Russian bishops, Shmuel Khan, and his brother Eshai, were murdered. Others were wounded. 46 bodyguards who were wounded were killed by the shameless traitor.

Afterward, another 48 fighters were killed when the stronghold of Simko Shakak in Chahar was taken.

After the bloody battle in Chahar, Simko and his followers fled to Khoi. In Khoi, there was a large number of Ashirat Assyrians from Tkhuma and some from Tyari and Mar Bishu. They were all refugees from Kurdistan. It is estimated that they numbered 4,000 individuals. All these Assyrians were massacred by the Kurds and the Afshars of Khoi.

Although there is no official record of the number of people massacred in Khoi, an estimate of 3,800 individuals is close to the facts.

It is noteworthy that the same way that the treacherous Simko killed the Patriarch together with 47 fighters of our nation, the Iranian army deceitfully killed Simko in 1930 in a feast in the town of Ushnuq, Kurdistan.

## The Battle of Assyrians with the Muslims of Urmia in the Surrounding Forts:

As said, at the time (1918) Urmia was under the control of Christians. But around the town, there were fortresses that were in the hands of the enemy, the Iranian fighters.

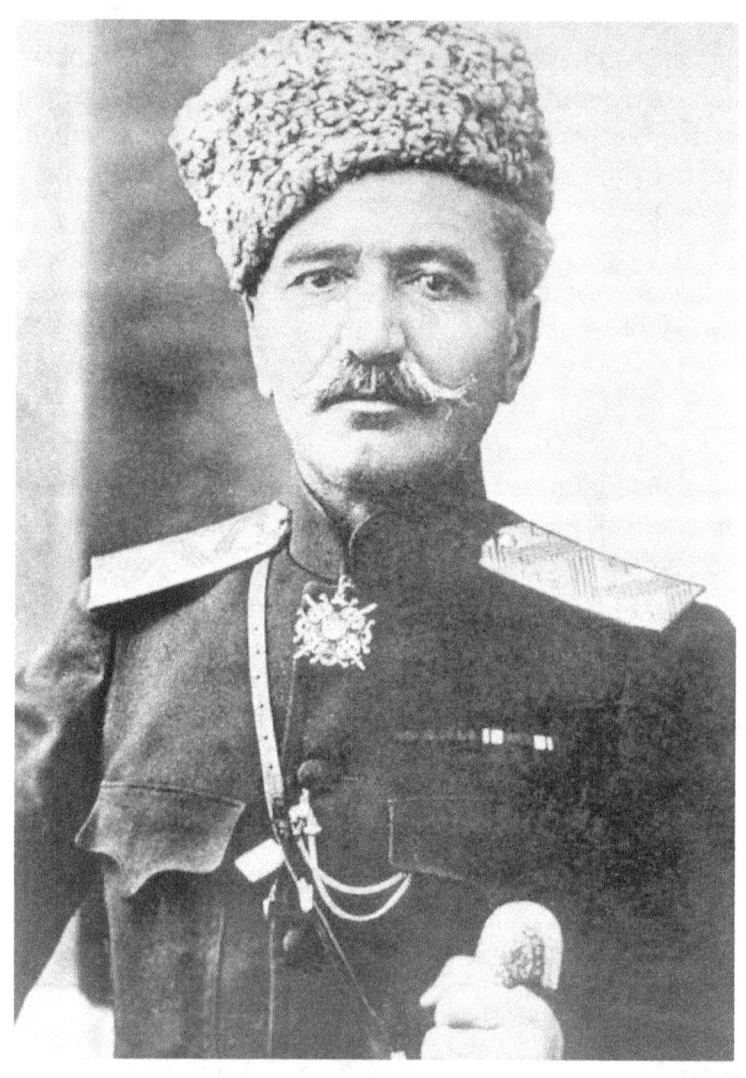

Andranik Pasha the head of the Armenian Military Force in Turkey

The citadel of Nassir-al-lah, a notable Iranian, was situated very close to the town of Urmia. Some of the Muslim fighters had blockaded themselves in that stronghold. Agha Petros sent a contingent of Assyrian fighters who laid siege to the fortress. The Iranian soldiers surrendered. In another fort owned by a lady called Gaysar Khanim, there were a group of Iranian fighters. They too surrendered after a battle of several hours.

Due to these successes, a part of the Assyrian battalion was dispatched to the village of Qassemluvi which is in a valley near Ushnuq on the Plain of Urmia. This was a large village with about 1000 families. It was under the control of Turks and Kurds. After a bloody battle, our fighters were victorious. But we lost six of our soldiers in that battle. A large number of prisoners of war were taken along with a sizable number of guns and ammunition.

During the last days of April-from April 23-28 in 1918, another fierce battle raged in Askarabad not far from the town of Urmia. This fortress was occupied by a large number of Kurdish and Afshar fighters fully armed. The Afshar fighters were known by the title "Qara Papaghi" [Black Caps]. After a violent battle of several days, The Christian powers took the fortress. Some of the enemy fighters were taken as prisoners of war, but a large number fled to the Kurdistan Mountains. Some of our soldiers were killed and some were wounded.

## Fierce Battles between Assyrians and the Turks:

In April of 1918 a part of our army was dispatched to Ushnuq to support the contingent we already had there to engage in a battle with the Turks. In the ferocious battle that ensued, the enemy was defeated. 13 prisoners of war were taken and numerous weapons were confiscated.

At the end of the battle of Ushnuq, another enemy force appeared from the north and skirted the village of Seir which was ten miles away from the town of Urmia. After a battle that lasted 8 days, the enemy was defeated. 350 prisoners of war were taken. Among them were two generals, and 24 officers, and a large cache of various sorts of weapons.

At the end of the month of April, the mobile French clinic under the supervision of Dr. Pauil Caujole that was stationed in Urmia back in February returned to Tabriz. The Russian consul, Basil Nikitine, returned with it.

Barely rested from the previous battles, our army was confronted with Division 5 of the Turkish army under General Ali Ihsan Pasha. This force came from Khoi and attacked Salamas. But again, with the help of the Lord, the enemy was defeated. Many were taken captive together with weapons of war. But on May 15, that same defeated Division of Ali Ihsan Pasha, with the help of the Division 7 of the Turkish army, attacked Salamas a second time. Right away we received help from Urmia to strengthen our fighters in the face of this large Turkish force. Even though our numbers were much smaller, again with the help of the Lord, we defeated the enemy and took 25 prisoners of war, a physician, and a lot of artillery. After this victory, the inhabitants of Salamas fled to the town of Urmia.

Among the prisoners of war, there was a soldier by the name of Ali Chavosh. He was an expert in the use of machine guns. Because the prisoners of war were taken care of well with respect to their food and sanitation, Ali Chavosh came to Aga

Petros and told him that he had been a loyal fighter for his army; but now that he had witnessed we were a brave and merciful nation, he was ready to join our forces and fight loyally with us on the condition that machine gun was returned to him. Agha Petros accepted the offer and ordered Ali's machine gun to be given back to him. Thus Ali Chavosh fulfilled his promise and fought with the Assyrians valiantly to the end.

When we reached Baquba, Ali Chavosh took a government post. He was sent to Akra where he married a native of Akra, the daughter or sister of Osman Yusef. Then he was transferred to Turkey. He left with his wife. According to his letter to his father-in-law, he was promoted to the position of an officer in Diyarbakir.

A large number of prisoners of war were brought to the American Mission compound. They were looked after well. The number of Turkish prisoners was over 400 individuals. These were added to the Mullahs and Mujtahideen that were already there which brought the total to 700. 1918 was a year of famine in Urmia. The prisoners were given rations of half a pound of raisins with a little bread each day. Many died of hunger.

## Andranik Pasha Sends Messengers to Urmia:

At a critical time in April 1918 Andranik Pasha, a famous Armenian general who had a 60,000 strong army in his command in Yerevan, Armenia, sends a letter with three messengers to the Assyrian and Armenian commanders in Salamas and Urmia to join him in Khoi. But the messengers never reached their destination. It is believed that they arrived

71

in Van where Levon Pasha was one of the Armenian commanders. What transpired there is not clear. While we were in Urmia in 1918, we learned that the messengers were detained by Levon Pasha.

When Levon Pasha was fighting the Turks, Andranik Pasha had tried to send him reinforcements; but the prideful Levon Pasha had refused assistance. As it happened his forces were completely destroyed in the battle with the Turks. Andranik Pasha was furious with him. In order not to be court-martialed, Levon Pasha had the three messengers who could serve as witnesses, killed on the pretext that they were not Armenian, but Turks.

This was unfortunate for our nation because the plan for a combined military force with Andranik Pasha did not materialize. Consequently, both fronts were weakened and even Andranik's strong military force was defeated.

To this day no one really knows what happened to the three messengers except the Armenians.

Soon after our initial victory over the Turks in the south, especially over Division 6 under the command of Haji Abraham Affandi, this division received reinforcements from the west from Division 12 under the command of Haydar Beg. The combined forces of these two commanders attempted another attack on our forces; but again with the help of almighty God, we drove back the enemy. We acquired weapons of war and took prisoners as well.

We were in a critical situation as we were facing a much stronger enemy. Agha Petros, with the advice of other military

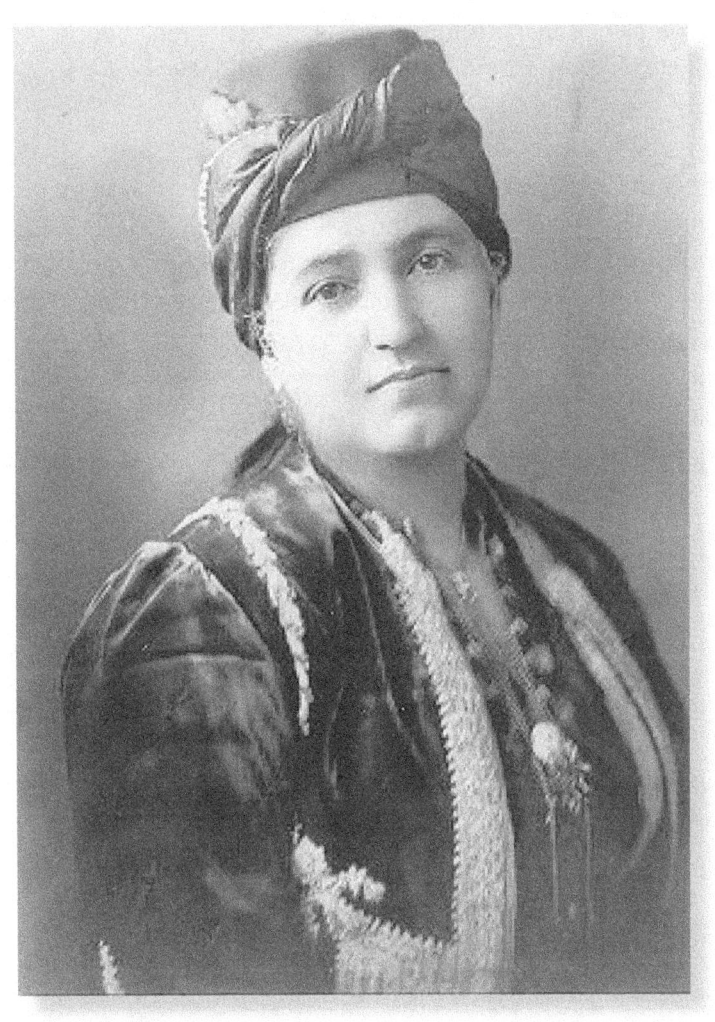

Surma Khanim the sister of Patriarch Mar Benyamin

leaders and the Armenian commanders, decided to withdraw our fighters closer to the outskirts of Urmia because there was no chance for the Assyrian and Armenian fighters to stand up to the sea of military forces against them even though the Christians had fought valiantly and had been victorious previously.

The Turkish prisoners of war were taken care of well by our forces. They were aware of the Assyrian humane treatment of prisoners of war. Therefore they came to Agha Petros and with the advice of their officers, told him that even though the Assyrians are a small nation, they have fought bravely, but will not be able to resist the Turkish forces. Sooner or later they will be defeated especially because the Allied Powers had deceived them. It was more profitable to make peace with the

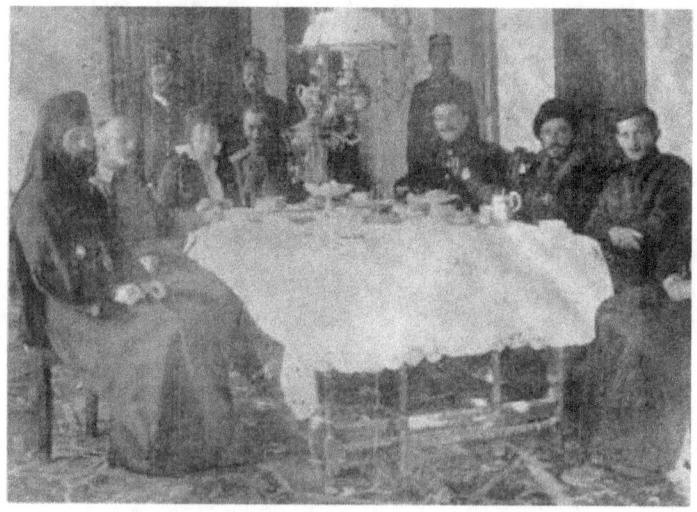

Patriarch Mar Benyamin in Urmia during the granting of the medal of Recognition. This picture was taken in the Russian Consulate in the town of Urmia in 1917. From R.-L. Basil Nikitine with Patriarch Mar Benyamin, Agha Petros, Colonel Tabureh, The wife of Basil Nikitine, General [Lodowiski], Mar Sargis the bishop of the Russian Orthodox Mission

Turks. They promised to be the go-between and negotiate with the Turks on behalf of the Christians. They assured Agha Petros that the Turks would receive their peace offering honorably and no harm would be done to them because the Assyrians are a brave nation, valiant, and merciful conquerors. Further, they made the point that the British friends, especially the Russians were not sincere and had their own problems. An armistice would assure the Assyrians the chance to return to their homes, salvage their possessions, and live in safety away from warfare.

But Agha Petros and other national leaders replied that it was impossible for them to surrender to the Turks. They preferred to be annihilated than betray their allies.

At the end of the month of June, we suffered heavy losses from Turks, Kurds, and others. A large number of our fighters were killed. But the Lord was helping us. We were ending up victorious and took prisoners of wars and weapons of various sorts. The captured soldiers were happy to surrender to our forces because their lives were spared and had enough dried squash in their bags to live on.

From 1917 to 1918 up to 14 attacks were launched against our forces. But with the grace of mighty God, they were all repelled. We must be thankful to God for saving us.

## 180 Assyrian Fighters Murdered in the Port of Sharifkhana in Tabriz:

Another calamity befell our forces when our weapons were depleted. We learned that the Russians had stored a large cache of weapons in the port of Sharifkhana on the other side of the Lake of Urmia, on the shore of Tabriz. The Assyrians selected 180 armed young men who left in a boat navigated by a German named Narman Khan. He was the son-in-law of an Assyrian family. He had married Rakhil Khanim, the daughter of Deacon Oraham of Urmia.

The Assyrians arrived in the port of Shaifkhana; but as rumored, Narman Khan betrayed the Assyrians and ran the boat into the marshes by the lake shore. Either that or the Boat got caught in the mud accidentally and could not be disengaged. The armed inhabitants of Tabriz arrived and apprehended all the Assyrians on board. They confiscated their weapons. After that, they paraded them in the streets. Then they returned them and killed them all at the Port of Sharifkhana.

The murder of the 180 fighters was not clear to us. Were these young men arrested after they fought the Muslims of Tabriz, or without a fight? Could it be that they were taken off guard, or did they run out of bullets? The incident remained obscured at that time. All the Christians were in mourning for this loss.

# Chapter 6

## The Condition of the
## Christians in Urmia
## A Plane on the Horizon of
## Urmia in July 1918

After all these agonizing experiences during the years of war in Urmia and in the mountains, an event took place that gave us the hope that deliverance was near. But the opposite happened. In a catastrophic turn of events, we were uprooted from our land, our homes, and almost our very existence was jeopardized.

It was on June 25, 1918 of the Eastern Calendar when all of a sudden an airplane was spotted on the horizon of Urmia. The Assyrians thought it was a Turkish airplane. So they bombarded it from every corner. The pilot kept waving a white flag until he found a landing field near the village of Sangar. The Assyrians ran to the plane and found out that the pilot was from the British Air Force by the name of Lieutenant Pilot Pennington. The Assyrians were very happy and took him with great honor to their leaders. A meeting was held headed by Agha Petros, the commander of the Assyrian army, and other leaders including Surma Khanim the sister of Patriarch Mar Benyamin, Dr. Shedd, the Director of the American Presbyterian Mission, and some Armenian leaders and Russian officers who, as I mentioned before, were there to assist us.

The pilot told the members of the committee that the Allied forces, especially the British were very grateful for our outstanding war effort; that the British expedition would arrive in Sayen Qala with arms of all kinds and abundant ammunition, clothing, food, and whatever else that was important to us. But they were asking 2,000 of our armed men to leave and reach Sayen Qala in a few days which was located 150 miles southeast of Urmia. The British expedition would then return with the Assyrian contingent to Urmia.

Some of the Committee members did not agree with this proposal; especially Dr. Shedd did not think it was advisable that 2,000 fighters leave Urmia. He used to say: "keep the Urmia front. The war is ending. You will be given rights in Azerbaijan because you have helped the Allied forces. (He was relying on the promises given by Captain Gracy when he came to Urmia from Tiflis on December 3, 1917. Captain Gracy was the official representative of the British military mission in the Russian Caucasus, and an official representative of his government. He made those commitments on behalf of his government in the presence of Patriarch Mar Benyamin who had just returned from Salamas, Basile Nikitine, the Russian Consul in Urmia, and Dr. Pauil Caujole, the head of the French Lazarist Clinic.

The captain repeated the promise that was given to the Assyrians regarding a home for Assyrians in Azerbaijan and in Hakkari[11] located in the Mountains of Kurdistan that would be under their own control.

---

[11]    Translator's Note: The Hakkari Mountains were the homeland of The Assyrian independent tribes, the Ashirats, for many centuries.

Sadly, the final vote was to join the British contingent in Sayen Qala. The Assyrians naively believed Lieutenant Pennington that they would soon be back with the British expeditionary force.

It is important to note that when we reached Hamadan after evacuating Urmia, the Assyrian Committee brought up the issue of the British promises to the Assyrians by Captain Gracy. But the British denied such promises. They claimed they did not know a person by the name of Captain Gracy to have made such promises. They claimed we had fought against the enemy to safeguard our families. Then it dawned on us that this was a British ploy to uproot the Assyrians from Azerbaijan and alienate them from Russians, the Assyrian first friends. The goal was to prevent the Russians from taking control of Azerbaijan either by Assyrians uniting with them or by them using the protection of the Assyrians as a pretext to occupy Azerbaijan.

Dispatching 2000 strong fighters away from Urmia at a time when our forces were fighting against a powerful army composed of Turks, Kurds, and others, was a catastrophic blow to the Assyrians and the Armenians.

According to the decision of our leaders and the advice of Lieutenant Pennington, on July 1. 1918 of the Eastern Calendar, 1800 armed cavalry men under the command of Agha Petros accompanied by Shlimun-d-Malik Ismael, Awu, the son of Shmuel Khan, Mar Yossip , Mar Sargis and others proceeded to Sayen Qala amid a ferocious battle. They reached their destination two days later than scheduled as they had to fight their way through the enemy line. When they reached Sayen Qala, they found out that the British contingent had retreated to the interior of the country. After contacting them by telephone, the British returned back to Sayen Qala and joined our forces.

## Malik Khoshaba Passing through the Mountains of Kurdistan on His Way to Mosul:

A short time before our exodus from Urmia towards Sayen Qala, Malik Khoshaba takes with him 12 armed fighters from Tyari. He makes his way to the Mountains of Kurdistan for the purpose of reaching Mosul and asking for assistance from the British. In a perilous journey surrounded by the enemy the men brave their way through the enemy line by sleeping during the day and walking during the night. Finally, they reach the monastery of Rabban Hormiz, a few miles north of Alqosh. There they hear that Mosul was under Turkish control [not that of the British].

Hungry, Thirsty, and exhausted, they make their way back through the same treacherous path. When they reach Urmia, they find out that the nation had fled the area. They find their way to Hamadan [where the nation was,] by threatening a guide to lead the way. There they meet the refugees and together, they proceed to Baquba.

Their journey back and forth takes more than 1000 miles.

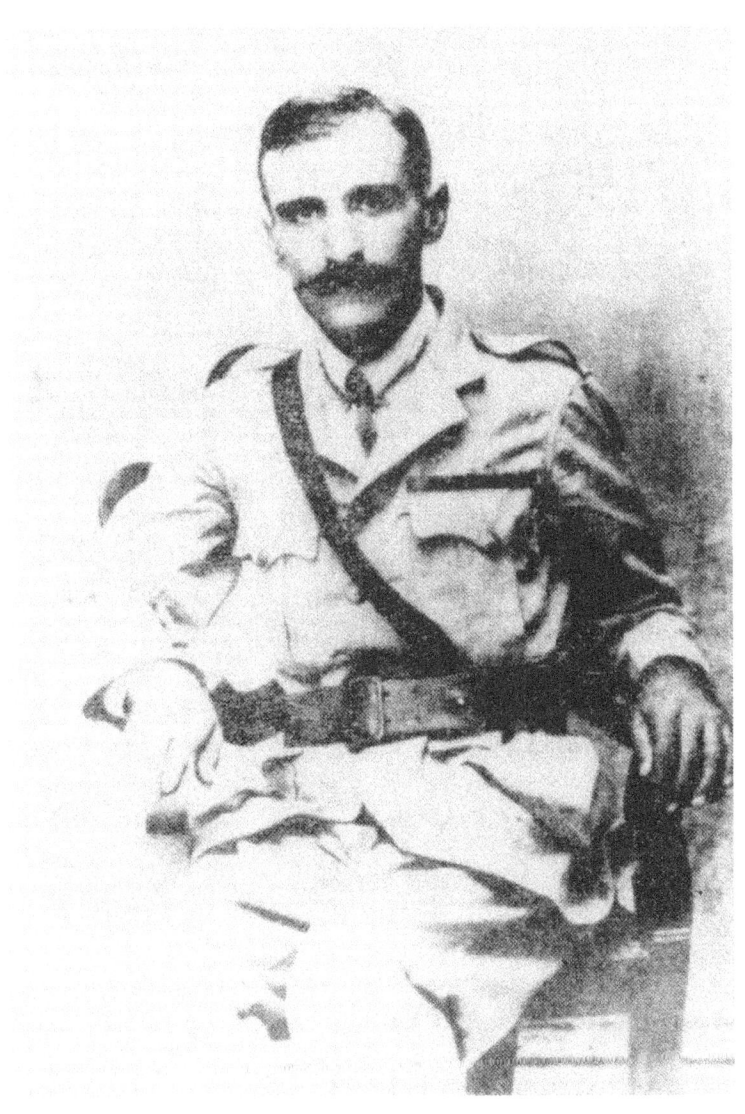

Malik Khoshaba of Lower Tyari

# Chapter 7

## Foreign Missions: Their Establishments in Iran and Elsewhere

In 1829 an American Presbyterian Missionary visited the Assyrians in Urmia and Kurdistan Mountains. He discovered that the Assyrians of these two areas lack literacy and education. They also are small in numbers and lack copies of the Holy Bible. Through him, other Presbyterian Missionaries established mission stations in Urmia as follows:

Starting in 1835 the first mission is opened under the direction of Rev. Justin Perkins and Dr. Asahel Grant.

In 1836 they opened the first school for higher education on the slopes of a mountain in the village of Seir, six miles north of the town of Urmia. After a short time, that school is promoted to the level of a college and relocated closer to Urmia on a large 15 acre tract of land. It is renamed "Qala-d-Sahabi" and is only two miles away from the town of Urmia.

From this college graduated students in the field of theology to serve as Presbyterian clergy in different villages. There were also graduates in the field of education as teachers, and in the field of medicine as physicians.

In 1838 a seminary was opened for girls by the name of "Fiske Seminary". In this school, girls were taught general education, in addition to various vocational skills as well as etiquette.

Occasionally Jewish and Muslim girls were also registered in this school.

In 1839 a printing press was acquired to print textbooks and other reading books. In the last quarter of the 19th Century, 58 books were printed on different subjects both in Swadai [The Assyrian Vernacular] and classical Syriac. A Holy Bible was printed in New York in 1851 which included the essentials of the Presbyterian theology.

In 1855 a monthly newsletter by the name of "The Rays of Light" was introduced.

In 1880 a large hospital was built. Its head physician was Dr. Cochran.

By the end of the 19th Century, the mission had opened 100 schools throughout many of the Christian villages. Even though the American Mission was also active among the Assyrian Ashirats residing in the mountains of Hakkari, its work did not spread widely as it did in Urmia. The exception was the village of Baz where there was a mission high school.

After that the American Missionaries opened mission stations in Hamadan, Qazvin, Rasht, and Kermanshah.

The French Catholic Missionaries, after establishing stations in Bet Nahrain like Mosul and some villages, also established Mission stations in Urmia and Salamas in 1839. They acquired a printing press to print books as well. In Salamas they opened schools for higher education for both boys and girls, and a theological seminary for young men to be trained for the priesthood. The French Mission did not make inroads among the Ashirats in advancing its denominational beliefs.

The French Missionaries started a monthly newspaper at the end of the 19th Century by the name of "The Voice of Truth".

After these came the Russian Orthodox Missionaries who opened a mission station in 1894 in Urmia. They spread their denomination very quickly. Within 23 years they became politically a powerful denomination. They expanded their mission into the Assyrian villages, and printed monthly newsletters. One was called The Orthodox Urmi; the other was titled The Light from the East"

They also opened a school of higher learning by the name of "Missia". They usurped many of the Church of the East sanctuaries by illegal means. Their work was not in the will of the Lord.

The other mission (before the Russian Orthodox) was the Episcopal Mission (The Anglican Church). This Mission was established in Urmia and also in the Mountains in 1884. It advanced and supported the teachings of the Church of the East.

With the support of the Anglican Missionaries, Classical Syriac became the language of writing and Swadai was left as the vernacular. The Catholic Missionaries also advanced Classical Syriac. But the Presbyterians dropped it after some time as they found it difficult to teach many different languages although they had included it in their curriculum initially. Consequently in the Qala College, the Fiske Seminary, and the Sardar College, the languages which were taught were Swadai, English, French, Russian, Farsi, and Turkish. Sardar College was established later for the education of the sons of wealthy Muslim leaders and Jews. Consequently Classical Syriac was abandoned in later years.

# Chapter 8

## Exodus from Urmia:
## On the Way to Sayen Qala

As mentioned in Chapter 6 a cavalry of 1800 armed Assyrian fighters left Urmia for the purpose of joining the British expedition in Sayen Qala. The departure of such a big force occurred at a critical time when Urmia was surrounded by enemy forces. Worse yet, Malik Khoshaba was far away in Kurdistan with 12 fighters in the hope of reaching the British contingent in Mosul.

The joint Turkish and Kurdish forces took the opportunity to attack from three angles. It became very difficult for us to maintain the Urmia front. We had run out of ammunition; and bullets. There was no forthcoming help. Our only help was God. An impending disaster was threatening the very existence of our poor, forsaken nation. So we were forced to flee Urmia on July 18 of the Eastern Calendar. We abandoned our homes, our ancient shrines, and villages and fled towards Sayen Qala to reach the British in order to escape a worse fate which was a total massacre by the Muslims who were thirsty for our blood.

Here, I give you a true testimony; that which I witnessed in person about our exodus from Urmia.

While sleeping on the roof of our house in Digala, we heard at night the noise of carts, the neighing of horses, and the commotion of men and women coming closer to our village from the direction of the town and the surrounding villages of

Urmia. This is because our village, Digala, is on the crossroad going from Baranduz River and Sulduz, to Sayen Qala.

On July 18 of the Eastern Calendar, we got up early in the morning having prepared a wagon to be drawn by two oxen loaded with food and other essentials. We left together with our neighbors and co-villagers abandoning our homes and possessions to the mercy of looters.

We were on the road with 70,000 other refugees in search of safety. We reached Geogtapa, about three miles away from Digala, in the afternoon of the first day. The roads were jam-packed with people and loaded animals. We had to wait for a long time in the fields of that village for our turn to cross over the bridge on the Baranduz River, which was 16 miles away from the town of Urmia. While waiting, all of a sudden we heard the noise of gunfire behind us. This was to frighten us and steal our belongings. So we decided to unload some of our belongings in order to be lighter and move faster as we fled in those dangerous circumstances. We threw a lot of our belongings in a stream and began to ride our oxcart more quickly. It was after midnight that we reached the bridge that separated Babarood from Darbarood. But the bridge over the river had collapsed because of the heavy carts and animals that had passed over it. The next morning of the second day of our journey, we found a way in the wider section of the river where the water was shallow and crossed from one end of the river to the other. We reached Haydar Abad in the afternoon of the second day.

This was an old harbor used by the Russian army. It was south of Lake Urmia. We stopped there to take a break. But after a short while, we were startled again by the sound of gunfire and enemy bullets aimed at us. So we got up and fled for the third day in a row until we reached a Kurdish village called Meehmatgar. There we stopped to rest a little. After a brief rest, we continued our trek and reached Miandoab. From there we continued on the way until we reached a large village called Qara Veiran on the fourth day. Again as we were resting in the streets and the open grounds of that village, those who were behind us were attacked from the west. And from the front, a bandit of Afshars and Kurds on horseback headed by one of our first assailants in Urmia, Majid-al-Saltana. But the Assyrian and the Armenian fighters under the command of Agha Ezaria of Ali-Kona and Ibrahim Khan who was a mighty Armenian military man were able to stop the enemy attacks after two hours of fighting.

Some women and children were killed in these attacks. Also, large amounts of goods and provisions, as well as wagons which were full of belongings, were carried away by the bands of murderers. To some extent that helped to clear the roads. The nation was on the move non-stop. But bullets were fired at us from here and there.

One morning around 10 O'clock before reaching Sayen Qala, we met nine British soldiers. One of them was an officer by the name of Captain Savage. They had "levis Ganna" in their hands and were coming to meet the end of the line of refugees. We were very glad to see them. But we were more eager to move on and reach our own army and that of the British expeditionary force in Sayen Qala.

It was near noon on the sixth day that we reached Sayen Qala. There we saw a few British soldiers with another officer named Captain Nicolas. We assumed that we were now safe from enemy attacks and terrifying incidences.

Some of our people had arrived a day or two before us. But there were others still on the way. People were arriving at a steady pace.

The 1800 armed fighters under the command of Agha Petros had reached Sayen Qala seven days before us. They were shocked when they saw that our people had fled Urmia and were arriving in Sayen Qala. But it was too late now, and the circumstances had turned against us.

We thought we could rest for a few days until arrangements were made to return back to Urmia with the help of the British forces and those of our own.

People had settled in the orchards. Food was being prepared. My mother was also preparing a meal so that we could have lunch in peace in the almond orchards of Sayen Qala.

Food cooked with "galya" [pre-cooked and preserved chunks of meat] and bread had sustained us thus far.

The meal was ready; but before we could sit down for lunch, suddenly bullets from gunfire rained upon our heads. They were again from the murderous band of Majid-al-Sultana. They were aiming at us from behind a hill on the north side of the village. They appeared to be on horseback shooting bullets at people.

But again our valiant fighters such as Rafael-khan, Awu the son of Shmuel Khan, Agha Ezarya, Awshalim Khan, and some others mounted their horses and chased the bandits who were thirsty for Christian blood. In a short time, they drew them far away from our people.

Again, without having had a meal, we got up and got ready to move on to the next stop, which was Deekan Tapa, from there to Bijar, and then to Hamadan.

In Sayen Qala there was a British contingent under Captain McCarthy. But it was not strong enough to overcome the enemy power and return us to Urmia, our beloved home base.

## Dr. Shedd, the Director of the Presbyterian Mission Passes Away:

We heard that Captain Reed was also in Sayen Qala with the British contingent. This was the same person who served in the Episcopal Mission in Urmia and sometimes in the Kurdistan Mountains.

Dr. Shedd, with his wife Mary Louise Shedd of the American Presbyterian Mission had also fled and had reached Sayen Qala. Dr. Shedd was exhausted from the four-year war in Urmia; especially during the period of time when the refugees were under his care in the American Mission compound. When we reached Sayen Qala, he became sick. Dr. Eshay Yonan of Geogtapa was treating him with medication. Within two days his condition worsened. The British army medical doctor, Peter Stone Hutch examined him a couple of times and gave him an injection against Cholera. Dr. Shedd did not wake up after this shot and passed away after a few hours. This was on July 26, 1918, on the Eastern calendar. He was born in Seir of Urmia in January 1865. His body was placed in a ditch and covered with dirt next to a rock. On it was drawn the sign of the cross in order to find the grave-site in the future.

As mentioned earlier, after the last attack of Majid-al-Sultana, we loaded our belongings and headed towards Hamadan, having lost hope of ever returning back to Urmia.

Henceforth there was no fear of enemy attack because the British and Indian army encampments were present on the road. Our own troops were with us as well. So we moved at our own pace and rested at night here and there in the fields and orchards on the way. After a few days, we arrived in Dikan Tapa, and then in Bijar. On the twentieth day after our exodus from Urmia, we camped in Taza Kand, a village west of Hamadan. This was because the British guards did not allow us to enter Hamadan, especially people like us who had oxcarts. A section of our people had taken a different route, and unknown to the British, they had entered Hamadan.

# Chapter 9

## The Condition of the 2000 Assyrians Left behind in Urmia after the Exodus of the Nation

Let us look at the condition of our people who were left behind after our departure from Urmia.

After we fled, we found out that about 2,000 Assyrians were left behind in the villages and the houses in the town of Urmia. Some were sick; some had no means to escape, and others were protected by their Muslim friends.

Afterward, some of these were killed by the Turks, Kurds, and Afshars of Urmia. About 100 were deported to Salamas by the orders of the Turks.

The reason for the deportation is not known to this day. Of these, only 300 survivors returned to Urmia after a few months. Another 600 came under the protection of the French Mission compound in the village of Golpatalikhan, Urmia. Only a few of these escaped torture and slaughter. The rest were murdered. Even the French Msgr. Sontag, the Pope's metropolitan was murdered with them on the order of Ashrat Homayoon as mentioned earlier.

In the month of October, that is, three months after our exodus from Urmia, Judith Khanim [Lady Judith], the wife of Kasha Yaccu David of Seir, with the help of Rabi Suriya, the wife of Rabi Youkhana Mushi (John Mushi, the school

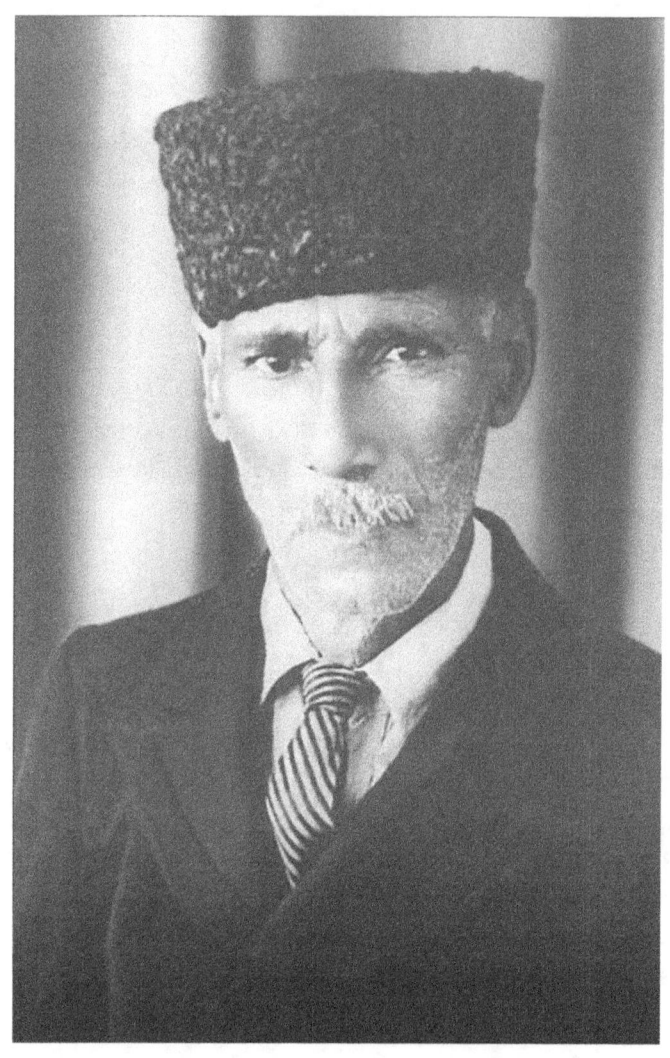

Rafael Khan, the Head of the Assyrian Military Force in Urmia

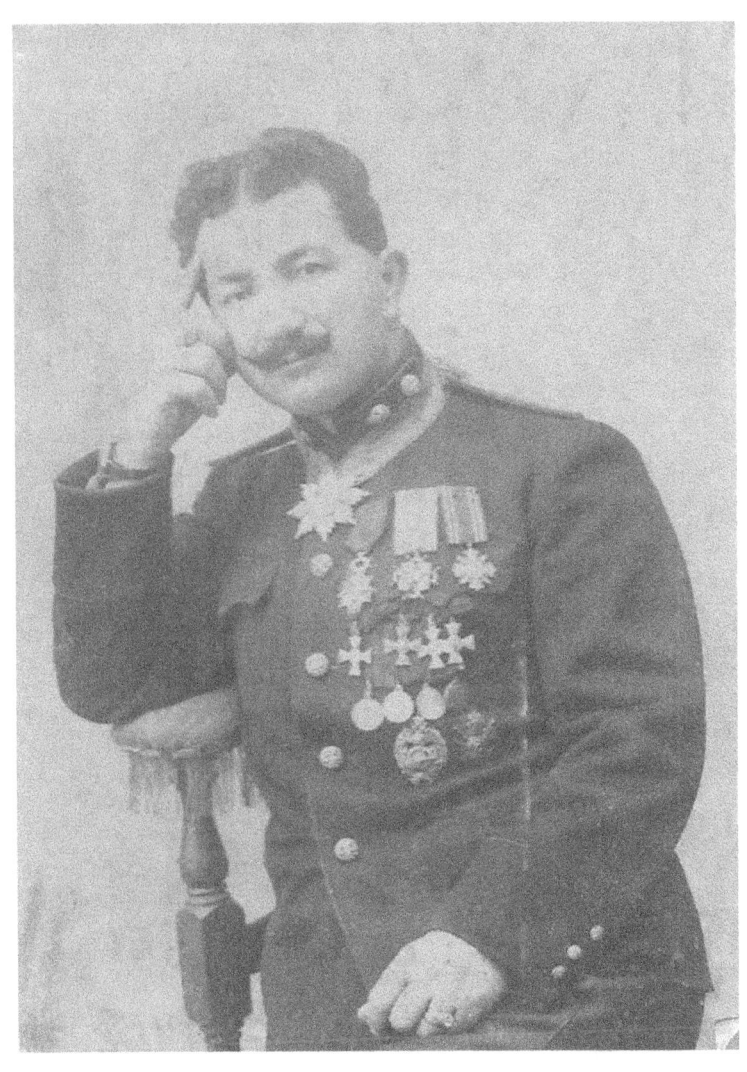

**Agha Petros**
Head of the Assyrian Military Force in Turkey and Iran

inspector), gathered 500 people from the villages and from the houses in town and brought them to the American Mission compound. They fed and took care of them as well as the ones already there. The Relief came from the American Committee for the Armenian and Syrian Relief in Tabriz. The arrangements were made under the direction of some Iranian authorities who were friends with Kasha Yaccu David.

At this point, it is worthwhile to note that Kasha Yaccu David was the director of the Sardar College in Urmia for some years. Generally, the students in this college were from elite Iranian families and some Jews. This college was financed by the American Mission. So even though these refugees were under the care of the American Missionaries, they were, nonetheless, protected by the Iranian elite families who were friends with Kasha David.

By May 24, 1919, the Turks had evacuated Azerbaijan because World War I had ended. But a fierce battle was raging between the Iranians and the Kurds. At this time some bandits entered the American Mission compound. 250 people were killed and about 100 wounded. The American flag was torn to pieces and trampled under their feet.

Some American Missionaries who had not left Urmia with us had stayed in Qala (Qala-d-Sahabi), a short distance north of Urmia. They were taking care of the sick in the hospital, and the children in the orphanage. After our exodus, these missionaries were stranded in that place and finally taken to detention centers by the Turkish soldiers. Most became sick of the lack of food and care. Pastor Herman Flomir who was the head of the orphanage, was murdered on the first day of our flight from Urmia. The rest were scattered here and there.

Dr. Ike P. Packard had gone to Tabriz with his family a few days before we left Urmia. When they heard that the Turks had evacuated Urmia, they thought that the town was safe. For this reason on May 6, 1919, they returned to Urmia. But a few days after their arrival, as mentioned earlier, a battle broke out between the Iranian forces and the Kurds. The situation became dangerous. Therefore, all the missionaries together with the rest of our people took refuge in the safe houses prepared for them by the Iranian government officials. They were supported for three weeks while there was an imminent danger to their life.

When the news about them reached Tabriz, The consul in Tabriz, Gordon Paddock, together with Pastor Ike I. Muller and Dr. I. Dodd took a top-ranking Iranian government official and a British driver with them. They drove in two cars from Tabriz to get help from Simko in Salamas. Simko provided them with a hundred armed fighters on horseback on the way to Urmia. There they took Dr. Packard and his family together with the 600 Assyrians and brought them to Lake Urmia to sail on a boat across the lake to Tabriz. In Tabriz, the Near East Red Cross took charge of these refugees.

Close to 800 Armenians who had taken refuge around Van from the Turkish onslaught, and those who were in hiding here and there in Azerbaijan, also found their way to Tabriz and came under the care of the Near East Relief.

# Chapter 10

## Exodus from Hamadan to Baquba, Bet Nahrain

When our people reached Hamadan, new promises were made to the Assyrians by the military officials of Great Britain regarding our repatriation to Urmia. An agreement was reached between Colonel J.G. McCarthy and our leaders to recruit our men to form a contingent who would be drilled and armed for the purpose of marching back and liberating our home base.

At this time the majority of our people were camped in Taza Kand in a large area close to Hamadan.

After two days of our arrival there, one afternoon two British guards came and began recruiting Assyrian young men to be drilled and trained for the purpose of liberating Urmia and other ancestral lands. I was enlisted together with many other young men. (I was 18 years old at the time.) We were taken to a village called Abshineh two hours away by foot south of Hamadan. When we reached there, we met about 1,000 Assyrian cadets who were gathered there for the same military purpose.

The next day we were summoned and lined up in military fashion. At this time we saw Agha Petros with some British officers. They began to record our names. Agha Petros was asking each person their name and that of their father. But before making a list of our names, Agha Petros gave a speech in which he said: "Dear Assyrian young men, you are brought

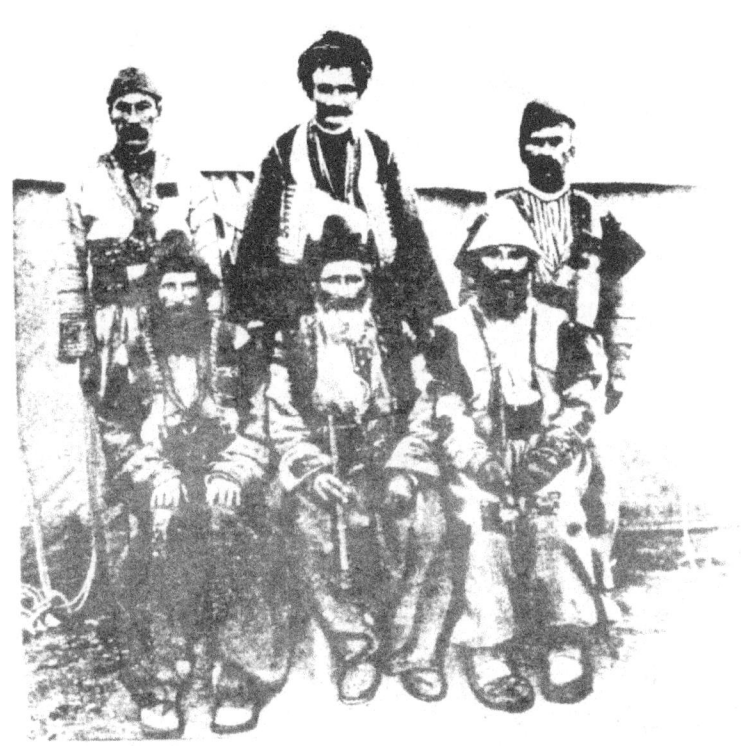

The Clergy and Deacons of the Church of the East in
Baquba in 1919

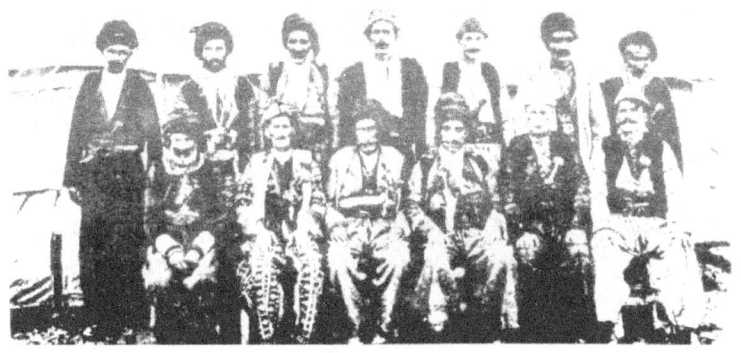

The Maliks and Leaders of the Ashirats in the Baquba
Refugee Camp in 1919

here to be trained for military service. We will, with the help of the British, return back and take over our former lands in Urmia and elsewhere."

After three months under the British military training, we were all led to Baquba, Bet Nahrain which was about 300 miles west of Hamadan, and 35 miles north of Baghdad. We were told that we must be taken to Bet Nahrain for further preparations and then return back to possess our ancestral lands.

We left Abshineh on a long journey of 20 days for Baquba. As soldiers, we were marching 15-18 miles each day. At the same time, our people were also being moved in groups to Baquba some on foot; others who were elderly or sick were loaded on carts driven by mules that were led by Indians.

When we reached Kermanshah, we rested by a river for one day near the high mountain of Bistun. There we met a large number of our people who were employed by the British to break rocks for one Giran [unit of Iranian currency] a day which is equivalent to one Rial today. There I asked the army officer permission for my parents to accompany me because I had the rank of a Sergeant. So my parents traveled with me up to Baquba. They were not on foot like us, but were carried on army carts.

As I mentioned earlier, we reached Baquba after 20 days. This was a large tent town. The British military personnel had prepared this large encampment for a number close to 80,000 Assyrian and Armenian refugees. The encampment was subdivided into 60 camps. Each camp had 50 large tents. In each tent lived no less than 25 individuals. There was a larger camp with larger tents set up as a hospital. Another one was earmarked for food preparation. There were other arrangements for shops, bazaars, etc.

But because of the dire conditions under which our people had traveled for such a long way, many people died in the first month of our encampment. There were 40-50 deaths each day.

A few months after our settlement in this big camp of Baquba, I think it was the first month of 1919, Aga Petros, who had been the commander of our army, and in charge of the protection of our people in Azerbaijan, was banished from the camp, separated from our nation, and together with his brother Aga Mirza was sent away to Baghdad. They were accused of causing dissension among our people. So our Urmia contingent was dismantled and we all returned to civilian life with our families in the camp. But the other battalion, composed of our Ashirat brothers from the Hakkari Mountains, remained in action. It was called the "Assyrian Battalion". The reason was whereas our group, the Urmia contingent, was to return to liberate Urmia and Salamas, the purpose of the Assyrian battalion was to procure a settlement for the Assyrians in Northern Iraq.

# Chapter 11

## Assyrians in the Baquba Camp, then Mindan

The banishment of Agha Petros did not sit well with our people. It caused a lot of anguish and hopelessness regarding our return to our home base. It was especially agonizing for the people of Urmia who had set their minds on returning back to their ancestral homes. Among them were knowledgeable and notable leaders who had served on the Urmia Committee of elders back home. They sent a petition to the British under the direction of Lieutenant Colonel F Cunliffe-Owen, the deputy of General Austin, who was the commander of the British forces in Iraq. The petition stated that Agha Petros had been a loyal and capable leader. "He fought heroically and saved our people from the enemy forces that had surrounded us with the intent of total annihilation. For this reason, we request that you examine this situation with kindness and return the general and his brother to be with our people. We hope that in your meetings and deliberations with him, you will reach a satisfactory plan to return us back to our former homes."

Before the return of Agha Petros and his brother to the camp, Colonel Owen used to come and give reports to the people. His report contained this message: "We, the British, cannot return you back to Urmia. It is as impossible as a child attempting to climb up the moon. The war has ended. The British have reached an agreement with the Iranians. We must withdraw all our forces from Iran." At such events, some of our women would become infuriated with the colonel's announcements especially because the British had brought Mar Timotheus from Malabar to be their spokesman and try to dissuade us from returning back to Urmia. Mar Timotheus began to give speeches in the camp telling the Urmia Assyrians: "Is it the memory of the sour grapes from your vineyards that is making you want to return to Urmia? Listen to the British. They will do you good. They will find you a better place than Urmia."

Such speeches increased the fury of the Assyrian women against Colonel Owen.

The British were giving up options to settle in a different country. They were giving us names of the countries like Cyprus, Brazil, Argentina, Canada, southern Africa, etc. But the Assyrians of Urmia kept insisting on returning back to their homeland. They protested saying "It is not sure if other countries will accept us. What if they do not?" Thus the problem was unresolved.

Finally the British relented and reinstated Aga Petros with the plan to return us back to Urmia. At the end of 1919 Agha Petros and his brother Agha Mirza were returned to the camp to reassemble the former battalion that had been dismantled several months before. It was to be armed and prepared to take possession of our home base.

Thus when Agha Petros returned, according to the agreement reached with the British and with the Urmia Committee members, as well as some Ashirat leaders such as Mallk Khammu-d-Baz, Malik Khsoshaba of the Lower Tyari, Malik Khannu of Tkhuma, and of course, with the consent of the people of Targawar, Margawar and Mar Bishu, he started to assemble the Urmia Battalion and to resume training and other preparations. But it was understood that we were solely responsible for this campaign. The British would supply us with weapons and we would be accompanied by two British officers whose duties were limited to being observers or reporters. The British would not be involved militarily in this expedition.

The arrangement caused conflict among our people. Malik Ismael of upper Tyari and other tribal leaders who were loyal to the Patriarchal family and were in the majority did not agree with this plan. They advised that we should wait for Surma Kanim's return from the Geneva Convention, and see what news she would bring us regarding the destiny of our nation.

I am not sure of the date Surma Khanim left for the Geneva conference. But I do remember that she was prompted to go to Geneva and give her vote so that Mosul would be given to the British and not to Turkey. This is because the Turks were protesting that The British had seized Mosul from Turkey after the end of World War I. And since the majority of the population was Turkish, that province must be returned to them. Needless to say, the Turks did not win this argument.[12]

The second point to be mentioned is that Agha Petros erected a memorial monument in the Baquba desert in memory of the 14,000 Assyrians who died during the two years we lived in this large refugee compound under the supervision of the British military forces. Most of the nation was present on the day of its inauguration and heard speeches by Agha Petros and the British officers regarding

---

[12]     Translator's Note: The Geneva Convention took place from 1922-1923.

the reasons for the memorial monument and reports regarding the preparations for the repatriation of our people to their ancestral homeland.

That monument was destroyed by the Arabs of the area after the camp was dismantled; except for its base that stands to this day.

A third meeting took place between Agha Petros and Colonel Owen. It was about the evacuation of the Baquba camp and relocation to Mindan camp which was 40 miles East of Mosul in the midst of low mountains near a small river called Khazal.

So on April 27, 1920 The Urmia Battalion partially armed, was loaded on train cars and driven to Baghdad. We landed in the Baghdad station and marched through the streets of Baghdad all the way to Mosul on the other side of the river. From there we went by train to Shirqat.[13] From Shirqat we went on foot for 6 days until we reached Mindan.

After two weeks the irregular soldiers, mostly from Targawar and Margawar, and others amounting to 1,500 fighters came and joined us in Mindan. After that came the Ashirats from Baz, the Lower Tyari and Tkhuma, and joined us. Finally, after a few weeks groups of families began to arrive. They were settled in the Mindan Camp.

## Clarification of a Misunderstanding:
I find it important here to write about an event that has been hidden from our people until today.

---

[13]    Translator's Note: Shirqat is the ancient city of Ashur

It was nighttime; maybe 10:00 PM. As soon as the train began to move towards Baghdad, a group from our platoon began to sing joyfully. Their joy was in anticipation of the return and takeover of our lost homes.

The platoon sang one or two stanzas from a military march composed by Sergeant Awshalim Abgar of Mart Maryam in Urmia. He had a pleasant voice and had the gift of composing military marches.

One week after we arrived in Mindan we heard that the Patriarchal family was very annoyed that we sang that song on the train when we left the Baquba camp. They had said "The Assyrians of Urmia were glad that Patriarch Mar Paulus Shimun passed away. That is why they were singing as they left Baquba."

This was a wrong assumption. I swear before God that we had not heard the news that Mar Paulus had passed away. It appears that he must have died a few hours before we left Baquba. Because on the same date that he passed away, that is, 27 of April, we also left Baquba. Had we heard the news, we would have of course, kept silent in honor of the Patriarchal family; since we always held the Patriarchal family in high esteem as the successors of an exalted office in our nation.

## The Arabs of Iraq: Riots against the British:

After we left Baquba, Arabs from different parts of the country began rioting against the British. They destroyed roads, toppled down bridges, and killed some Indians that were in the British military service.

They were also opening gunfire on the people still in the Baquba camp. Some had climbed on date trees that were on the other side of the river and were shooting bullets at the people. This was a time when the other Ashirat battalion was relocated to Abu Sef near Mosul and was not there to protect the camp.

The British had distributed some weapons to young Assyrian fighters and to the Indian soldiers who had lingered in the camp. Gradually this group was able to subdue the attacks on the camp.

Another time a train wagon was carrying weapons from Baghdad to rearm the fighters in Baquba. But because the railroad was destroyed before the arrival of the train, some wagons were derailed and their contents disclosed. The Arabs began to steal the weapons. The Assyrians arrived soon and quickly dispersed the bandits. Then they loaded the weapons onto a wagon and pushed it manually until they brought it safely to the camp.

After some time the rest of the families who were still in the Baquba camp, were relocated to Mindan. Then the Ashirats, especially the tribe of the Upper Tyari, were returned to settle in Southern Kurdistan in the villages of Nafkour, the district of Aqra.

Two months after we had settled in Mindan, some 200 of our regular company of soldiers were sent to Joujar located between Mindan and Aqra. They were there for two months when suddenly a joint force of two Kurdish tribes under the leadership of Rajab Obeidollah and Muhammad, the head of the Sirukhs, attacked them. A fierce battle ensued in Sept 17 until Sept 18, 1920 in which our fighters defended themselves vigorously. In the end, the Kurds ran away leaving behind some dead and some wounded. There were also large flocks of sheep which our soldiers took and delivered to the care of the British.

Among us was a British sergeant with an imposing figure. When the battle broke out, fear overtook him and the poor fellow lay in bed feverish all night long.

At this time one part of our force was in Aqra. But the larger part was in Mindan. We were all anxious to move towards Kurdistan on our mission to liberate Urmia.

# Chapter 12

## The Expedition to Kurdistan and Return to Mindan in Failure

On October 21, 1920, the Urmia battalion plus 1,500 irregulars (Drushineh) including those from Targawar, Margawar, and Mar Bishu together with the fighters of Malik Khoshaba of Lower Tyari and those of Malik Khammu of Baz, the troops of Malik Khannu of Tkhuma, and some Jilus composing a total army of 5,000, marched towards Kurdistan.

The primary purpose of this expedition was to reach Urmia under the command of General Agha Petros as the commander of the whole army. With him were high-ranking officers such as his brother Agha Mirza, Malik Khoshaba, Awu-d-Shmuel Khan, Rafael Khan, Agha Ezaria, and some other tribal leaders. We were in the rank of the officers of the Urmia Battalion. With us were two British officers in the role of observers. One was Captain Gibson; the other, Captain Homizd.

As soon as we passed Aqra, the orderly ranks of a supposedly disciplined army broke down and all fighters whether they were regulars or irregulars began to go their own way.

I was a two-star officer in the army. When we reached the Big Zab River ready to cross, I saw with my own eyes how seven soldiers drowned in it. The waters of the Big Zab were so rapid and torrential, that they knocked down those soldiers and carried them with their weapons on their shoulders to the middle of the river. They could not stand up and were dragged speedily under the water and drowned.

The British officers had given each one of the Assyrian officers a mule, a small tent, and two-foot soldiers from our own platoon to serve us. We were staring at the turbulent waters of the Zab afraid to step into the river.

Finally, we decided to cross the Zab. We tied our bundles and weapons on the mule, and the three of us held on to the tail and the saddle of the mule and crossed to the other side safely, with the help of the Lord. Others were holding hands while crossing the river.

After crossing the river, we began walking on a narrow and very long trail following those who knew the topography of the land. Very late one afternoon we reached a Kurdish village. The village was empty of its inhabitants. The houses were vacant. We found some molasses, fig bread, and berry bread in some houses. We bought some from those who had arrived there before us. They had collected these supplies and sold them to the late arrivals. For many days our diet consisted of fig and berry bread. Some days we boiled black beans and ate them without meat, oil, or salt.

One morning we got ready and continued our trek through the mountains and hills until we reached close to the village of the Zibar tribe. There we encountered many Kurds who were firing on those who had arrived there before us. We retaliated. This turned into a fierce battle. We defeated The Kurds. But the next day another ugly battle raged between us and an Artoush tribe. The Kurds were defeated again and ran away. But after two days, they attacked us a second time. We were firing at them from behind some cliffs. We were positioned on the slope of a mountain where the village of

Nirwa of the Soto Ashirat was located. A group of Kurds found the opportunity to sneak by and stabbed to death one of our officers with their daggers. His name was Gewargis Margus of Mawana. Eventually, they too were defeated and ran away in retreat.

In the middle of the battle torrential rains poured down on us as we fought and defeated the Kurds.

We raised our tent on top of a hill. My platoon of 50 soldiers took shelter under that tent as it rained all night long.

We stayed two days in Oramar to rest. We hoped that the morning after we would move forward and cross the Big Zab River to the other side where from the top of a hill the pastures of Targawar and Margawar could be seen, not too far from Urmia.

But in Oramar one evening Agha Petos gathered all the officers in his tent and said "Sons, we have to return to Mindan." This statement startled us. We were surprised to hear this sad news.

He told us the reason was our brothers the Ashirats of Tkhuma and Lower Tyari did not want to come with us to liberate Urmia. They had gone their separate way to take their own tribal lands. "For this reason, I do not see it advisable for us alone with a small force to confront much stronger powers and be able to take possession of our ancestral homes especially now that the winter freeze is approaching. Therefore, I am saddened to say we need to return back."

This news was devastating to us. After all that we had been through the horrors of exile, sickness, death, hunger, thirst,

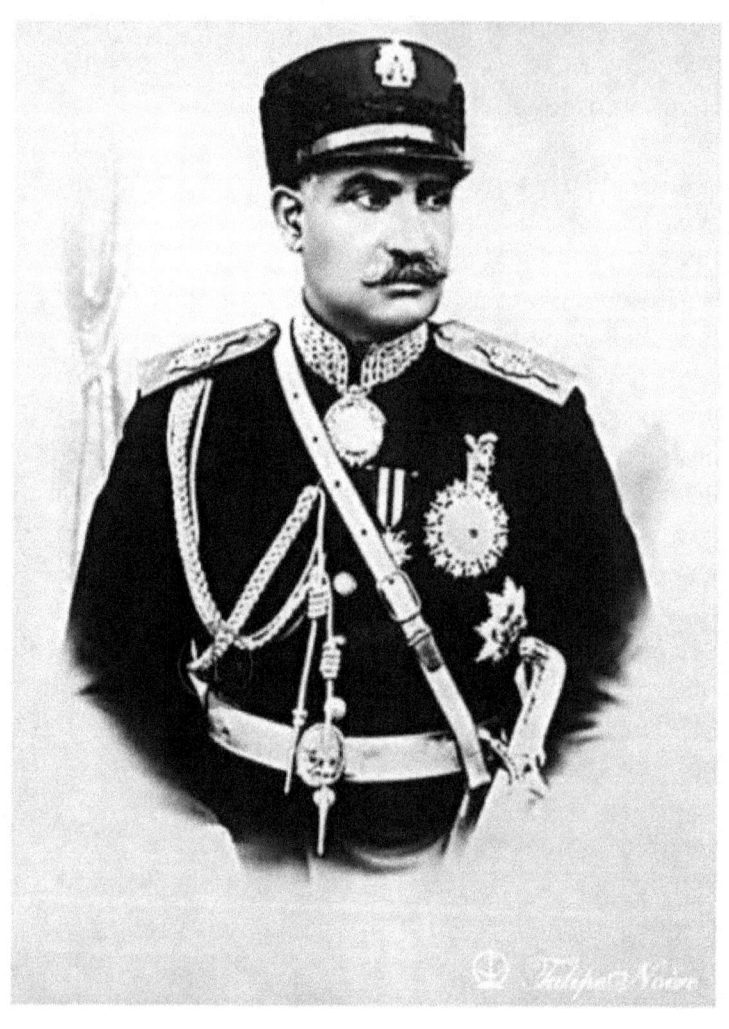

**Reza Shah Pahlavi**
the King of Iran during his Reign 1925-1941

and now the only hope we had left to return back to our former homes was dashed.

All the officers left the tent with a heavy heart and reported the sad news to the soldiers. They were devastated as well.

The next day we got up grief-stricken, tired, and feeling defeated. We took a different route towards Mindan. On the way, we passed over an old, narrow, and shaky bridge hanging over a river. After some days we reached Mindan with heads down and dejected as a defeated army.

Before reaching Mindan, we met a procession of men and women who had walked for two miles to meet us. Everyone was anxious to see their husband or son. For some families, the worst part was to face the bitter truth of a family member being killed, drowned, or fallen sick.

Sadness and desperation stayed with the people for a long time.

One of the British officers, Captain Gibson committed suicide when we reached Jujar. Because he found out we had lost many mules and weapons. The other Officer, Captain Homizd went to Mosul to report to Colonel Owen, the supervisor of the Urmia expedition.

The rest of us who were from the Urmia Battalion, delivered our mules, weapons, and tents to the British. We were then discharged from military duty and returned to civilian life with our families for the rest of that winter in Mindan.

## Agha Petros: Banished by the British from Iraq, on His Way to France

After the failed mission in Kurdistan, Agha Petros returned to Mosul a broken man. After a short time, the British banished him from Iraq. He left for France and lived with his family in Toulouse, a town south of France. He passed away from a heart attack in 1932.

His brother, Agha Mirza had gone to visit some friends in Tel Kaif. On his return, his loaded gun went off in the car. The bullet entered his body and killed him.

## The Assyrians of Urmia Request the Government of Iran to Return to their Homes:

In May 1921 the Assyrian Committee of Urmia sent a telegram to Reza Khan who was the minister of defense in Iran. At that time, Ahmad Shah, the Iranian king was sick and was hospitalized in France and Reza Khan was the acting Shah in his place.

The request of the Assyrians of Urmia from the Iranian government was: "We request that the gracious government of our country grant us permission to return to our former homes and live there as loyal subjects of the country."

The response of Reza Khan, as the leader of the country, was: "You are the sons of this country. Whenever you return to your homes and farms, you will be welcomed back."

Then the Assyrian committee of Urmia asked the British to release them from British custody.

Office of the Director of Repatriation
CIVIL Administration of Mesopotamia.
M O S U L.   11th.   July.   1921.

TO.

UROM WHOM IT MAY CONCERN.

_____Urmi Assyrian Refugee and family
of 5 Persons have received Government money grant and have
left Mindan Camp on their own responsibility, they are struck off
the strength of the Repatriable Assyrians from 12. 7. 1921.

Lieut.

For Lieut-Colonel.

Director of Repatri tion.

Countersigned_____
(head of family).

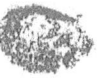

ܠܲܐܘܢܵܬܵܐ ܕܝܼܠܵܢ ܦܘܼܩܕܵܢܵܐ ܕܠܲܐܒܘܼ ܕܝܼܠܲܢ
ܡܸܢ ܒܸܝܬ ܐܲܣܝܼܪܘܼܬܵܐ ܕܐܸܢܓܠܝܼܫܵܝ̈ܐ
ܒ ܡܲܫܪܝܼܬܵܐ ܕܡܝܼܢܕܵܢ 1921

Copy of our Release from the British Custody,
at Mindan Camp June, 1921

113

After some months, the resolution of the British was that all Assyrians are free to take responsibility for their own life. They will be paid a certain amount of money for travel expenses, etc.

The Assyrians were happy with this response. Each person received 122.50 Rupees.

They signed a document stating every Assyrian has willingly relinquished the custody of Great Britain and is responsible for his/her own destiny. This document was signed on July 11, 1921.

Our Ashirat brothers who had left us while we were in Kurdistan, together with the rest, lived in villages with the intention of returning to their former homes.

Most of the Urmia Assyrians went to Baghdad. From there some returned to Iran. We made an arrangement with a number of families to sail from Mosul to Baghdad on the river rafts called "Kalaks".

It took six days to reach Baghdad. Kalaks are made with long logs tied together and set on inflated skin pouches. They are placed on the river and driven by the river currents.

# Chapter 13

## Assyrians in the British Military Service
## The General Condition of the Assyrians in Iraq

Soon after we had left the Mindan camp, Dr. William A. Wigram, a minister of the Episcopalian Church of England had come to Mindan camp and had visited the Assyrians in the villages of southern Kurdistan encouraging the young men to enlist in the British army. This was in the first days of April 1921. Our Ashirat brothers readily enlisted under the leadership of David Effendi, the Father of Patriarch Mar Eshai Shimun. A battalion of 4,000 fighters was formed.[14] Some of the officers in this regiment were Zia-d-Malik Shamsadin of Lower Tyari, Yossip Yokhanan Khiu of Rumta, Daniel and Yaccu, the sons of Malik Ismael of Upper Tyari, Agha Ezaria of Ali-Kumeh, and others.

The main purpose of this military force was to end uprisings in Kurdistan and drive the Turks far from the area.

In 1922 the tribes of Upper Tyari and Lower Tyari joined forces and returned to tribal lands and began to repair their houses and live in them. After 2-3 years the Turks sent a Vali [governor] accompanied by some soldiers to investigate why these people were living in the area without permission from the Turkish government. This is because this territory which was the ancestral home of our Ashirat brothers was now ceded to the Turks. Therefore, residence there without the

---

[14]     Translator's Note: The reference is to the Assyrian Levy.

knowledge of the Turkish government was not feasible.

Before the arrival of the Vali and his underlings in Tyari, the Tkhumnai had blocked their way and shot and wounded the Vali. They had also killed some of the soldiers. Then they had taken the Vali and his soldiers to Mosul to turn them over to the British. On the way, they had met Malik Khoshaba who set the Vali and his men free. The Vali went and reported the incident to the Turkish central government.

So, in 1924 Turkey sent an army against these Ashirats. The Ashirats were driven away from their homes a second time and had to return to Iraq.

Some of our people stayed in Iraq. They found jobs and started working. Many families as mentioned before, returned to Iran. Some settled in Kermanshah, Hamadan, Kazvin, Tabriz, and gradually a lot of them made their way to Urmia and Salamas.

When we stayed in Baghdad, some of us found jobs on the railroad, or in the oil fields; as the extraction of the "black gold" was becoming an industry.

## A Bloody Fight between the Assyrian Soldiers and the Muslims of Kirkuk:

On May 4, 1924, an ugly incident occurred in Kirkuk between some Levi Assyrian soldiers and some shopkeepers. The outcome was 178 Muslims, and three Assyrians dead, not counting the wounded.

A woman by the name of Rabcca, the wife of Sargis Kina

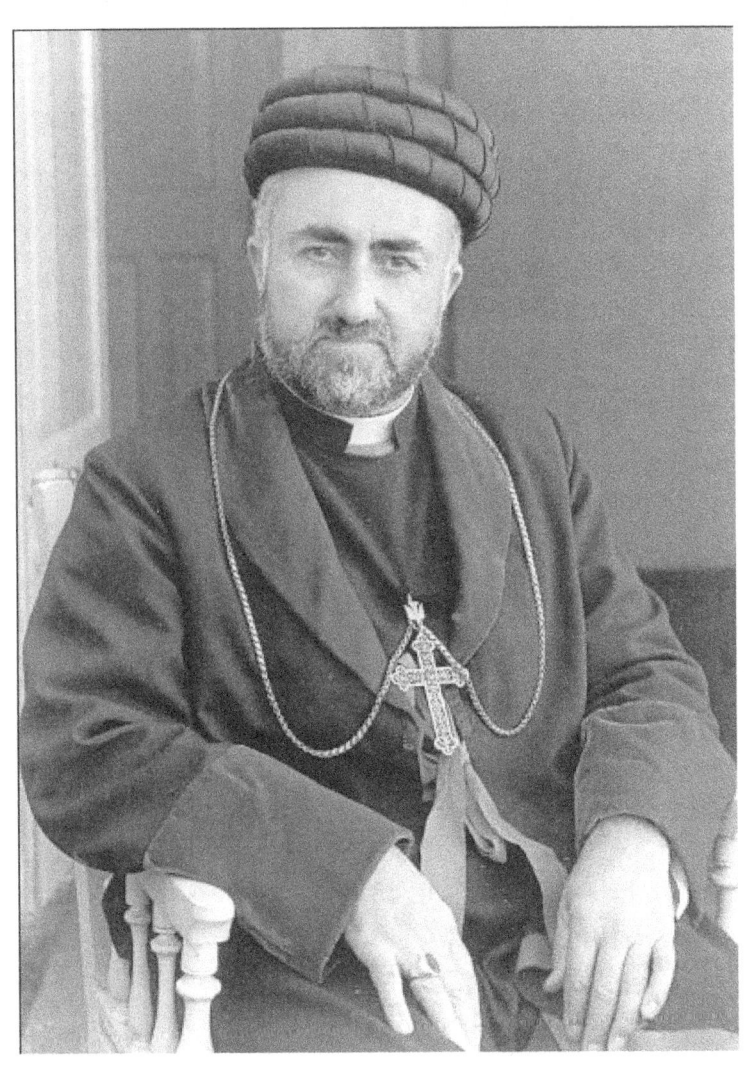

Patriarch Mar Eshai Shimun

Shimun of Qudchanis who had bought a kilo of sugar from a Muslim shopkeeper, had come to return the sugar because it was dirty and she did not want it. There was a dispute between her and the shopkeeper. After some Yay and Nays, the shopkeeper had spitted into the sugar, invoked a curse against the devil, and thrown the sugar into the street.

Accompanying this woman were a Yezidi and three Assyrian soldiers. (Yezidis are devil worshipers.)

The Yezidi was offended since his religion was insulted. So he began to beat the shopkeeper. Other shopkeepers came to the defense of their co-religionists. As the squabble became fierce, the Iraqi police got involved on the side of the Muslims. At this point, the Assyrian soldiers went and got their guns and began firing at the Muslims. Due to the severity of the fight, British soldiers were flown in on a plane and they subdued the fight.

On the same day, the Assyrian battalion which was in Kirkuk was removed from there and sent to Chamchamal, four Kilometers away from Kirkuk. Afterward, some of the individuals who had taken part in this fight such as Ezaria Tamuz, Magsud, Nikho of Tkhuma, Rab Khamshi Aprim Shawoul-d-Kelaita of Mar Bishu, and Corporal Gewargis Zkharia were all tried and imprisoned in Baghdad for one year. Moreover, everything that belonged to that Battalion was sold and with the sale of it, plus one day salary of the soldiers in that battalion, was given as indemnity to the families of the 178 dead Muslims.

One person by the name of Gewargis Zkharia who was one of the imprisoned men was killed on the Fallujah Bridge in 1941 during World War II.

## The Release of Assyrian Levy from Military Duty

In 1931, all of Kurdistan was cleared from Turks and Kurds by the Assyrian Levy. In a span of ten years, 1921-1931, the districts of Zakho, Rawanduz, and all the way to Suleimaniya were cleared. At this time Iraq attained complete independence. But the British forgot their promise about the Assyrian rights. For this reason, the two Assyrian companies that were left in the British service decided to leave the British and be free of it.

But it appears that new promises were made and on the recommendation of the Patriarch, they remained in the military service for one more year.

Then, in 1932 the two remaining battalions still in service were set free as well, except for a small number of personnel that were kept in Hinaidi to safeguard the British airplanes. The void in the Assyrian army was filled by the Arab army.

## Patriarch Mar Eshai Shimun Invites the Tribal Leaders to a General Council

In May 1932 Patriarch Mar Eshai Shimun invited the Assyrian tribal leaders, high clergymen, and Assyrian notables to a meeting in Sar Amadiya. As we understood this meeting was on the subject of the future of the nation.

A second council took place in June. The final resolution was to petition the governments of Great Britain and Iraq to settle the Assyrians in the mountains of Hakkari with Dohuk as the center. It was also resolved that the Patriarch should go to Geneva and present the Assyrian demands to the Geneva Convention.

In October 1932 the Patriarch went to Geneva and presented the resolution of the Assyrian tribal leaders and notables in the Geneva Convention. But he returned empty-handed and disillusioned.

Malik Yaccu on pages 203-214 of his book Assyrians between the Two World Wars mentions that after the departure from the Geneva Convention, a different petition was sent by a different group of Assyrians to the Geneva Convention that contradicted the Patriarchal demands. Those who signed that resolution were:
1. Mar Sargis the bishop of Jilu,
2. Mar Yab-alaha the bishop of Lower Barwar,
3. Malik Zaya-d-Malik Shamsadin of Lower Tyari,
4. Zadok Shimunaya, of Upper Barwar,
5. Malik Khammu Baznaya,
6. Kasha Gibrael Baznaya,
7. Malik Chikko Givu of Upper Tyari, and
8. Malik Odishoo of Upper Tyari.

So, on May 4, 1933, the Patriarch returned to Mosul empty-handed and disheartened.

During that summer, at a time of indecisiveness due to the disputes between the Assyrians and the Iraqi government, some British officials such as Major Thompson, the British delegate to the Paris Peace Conference, Lt. Colonel R. S. Stafford, administrator inspector in Mosul, and Khalil Azmi, Mutassarif[15] (Iraqi government official), tried to set a meeting and bring reconciliation between the two opposing Assyrian parties. But a bigger dispute erupted when each party tried to prove that its position was right and better for our people.

---

[15] Translator's Note: Mutassarif is governor.

On the other hand, we learned that on June 14, 1933, about 900 armed Assyrian fighters from those who were released from the British military service, headed by Malik Yaccu, had left for Syria. At that time Syria and Lebanon were under French rule.

The French had disarmed the refugees and granted them temporary residence until an agreement between them and the Iraqi government could be reached with the British as mediators.

So, one part of the group of Assyrians decided to return back to Iraq now that the French had not granted them permanent residence and join their families which they had left behind in the villages. The other group preferred to wait and see what would happen.

The former group who were in the majority got their weapons back; and on August 5, began to return by crossing over the Tigris River to the Iraqi side.

There was a big military Iraqi camp, the camp of Dairabun on the side of Zakho in the Iraqi Tkhuma. A part of the group crossed over and fought their way with the Kurds here and there through the mountains and hills until they reached their villages and families.

But a larger section came under fire from the Iraqi soldiers of the Dairabun camp as they were crossing over the river. A bloody battle broke out.

It is not known up till now who fired the first bullet. 45 Iraqi soldiers died in this battle and undoubtedly there were Assyrian casualties as well since the battle lasted two days.

Those who stayed with the French were 4 people. They were Malik Yaccu, his brother Shlimun, Loko Shlimun and Esho-d-Kelaita. These four people requested the French to grant them refugee status. The families of these refugees were under the observation of the Iraqi police in Iraq. (In a different place Malik Yaccu states that 550 fighters had stayed in Syria and had not returned to Iraq.) It appears that after the fight they must have returned to the French in Syria.

## Some Assyrians Deported to Nassiriya as a Punishment

The Iraqi government deported the following Assyrians to Nassiriya in southern Iraq on August 6, 1933. They were exiled away from their families and their people on the pretext that they were causing insurgency in the country.
1.  Malik Andrius Warda of Jilu
2.  Zkharia Kashisha Eshai-d-Kelaita
3.  Alexandrus Dashto-d-Kelaita
4.  Malkizdik Shlimun-d-Malik Ismaeil
5.  Malik Sawa warda of Taal
6.  Gewargis Haji of Chaal
7.  Kashisha Eskhaq Bar Kashisha Raihana
8   Kashisha Ablakhat Min Bar Hada

After some Assyrian notables were branded and punished as insurgents and sent to Nassiriya, the fury of the government officials against the Assyrians increased even more. At this critical time King Faisal I was sick and hospitalized in Switzerland. His regent was his son, the Crown Prince Ghazi, a young inexperienced man with a hot temper. The commander of the army was a Kurd by the name of General Bakir Sidqi. He was a German Nazi sympathizer and disliked the Assyrians.

It was rumored that Prince Ghazi was under the influence of Bakir Sidqi. Some of the high government ministers were also Kurds. It appears that they all plotted to take revenge against the Assyrians for the death of their men in the Iraq-Syria incident, by entering the Assyrian village of Simele and the surrounding villages and murdering young and old indiscriminately. Iraqi police stations were present in these villages to maintain law and order.

So, on August 11 the wounded Iraqi militia of the Western Iraqi army under Haji Ramadan, returned from the borders of Syria in a frenzy. It moved towards Simele, and brutally massacred 400-450 people indiscriminately. Inhabitants of other villages were alarmed and took refuge with their Arab and Kurdish friends.

Shamasha [deacon] Gewargis Benyamin of Ashita in his book Life in Tyari states that 250-300 were murdered in Simele; the majority were Assyrians from Tyari and Baz.[16]

## Patriarch with His Family Deported from Iraq Sent to Cyprus

After the atrocities that took place in the north of Iraq, the Christians in all of Iraq became apprehensive and troubled. On August 18, 1933, at a time when the nation was in mourning, the British took the Patriarch who was under house arrest in the YMCA in Baghdad and deported him to the island of Cyprus in the Mediterranean Sea. After a few days, the rest of the Patriarchal family who lived in Mosul were taken to Baghdad and from there to Cyprus.

---

[16]    Translator's Note: Patriarch with His Family Deported from Iraq

123

The Patriarch went to Geneva to submit his petition for the settlement of Assyrians to the Geneva Convention. Then the family left for England. After a few years of residence there, the family immigrated to the USA, the country flowing with "milk and honey".

The plight of the Assyrians became known worldwide through newspapers and other media. First, the Beirut newspapers wrote about the predicament of the Assyrians. This was followed by the media in the rest of the world who blamed the British and Iraqi governments for the devastation wrought on the Assyrian Christians.

The Assyrian case was discussed in the Geneva Convention. The final resolution was the families of those who had crossed over into Syria, must be moved there at the expense of the Iraqi government. Then Major Thompson, the British delegate in the Geneva Convention, opened an office in Mosul and one in Baghdad and began to register the names of the Assyrian families of those fighters that had left to Syria. Later the registration became open to all the Assyrians who wanted to move to Syria.

Thus, many Assyrians, mostly our brothers from the Upper Tyari and Tkhuma tribes applied to move to Syria. In general, those of the Lower Tyari did not move and settled in the district of Amadiya. Another village, Dadosh of Upper Tyari under Malik Chikko, also refused to move. They settled instead in Kora Gavana in the district of Dohuk on the road to Amadiya.

This created further divisions and conflicts among those who

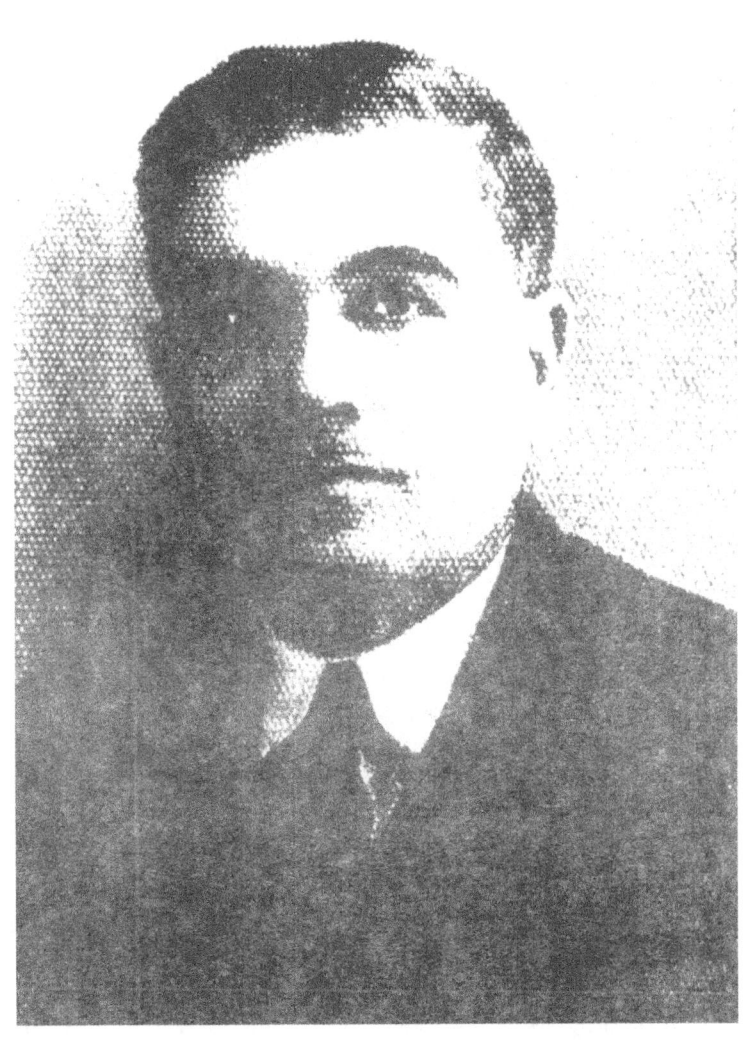

**Rev. Khando Hurmizd Yonan**
the Pastor of the Assyrian Evangelical Church in Baghdad

wanted to stay in Iraq and those who wanted to leave. The ensuing conflicts affected all the Assyrians even those who lived in Baghdad. The Assyrians in Urmia were also shaken to hear about yet another partition of the nation.

It is regrettable that a lot of discord was created in the nation because of differences of opinion among the people on this issue.

The members of the Assyrian Evangelical Church in Baghdad also heard about the move to Syria. The pastor of the church, Qasha Khando Yonan of Tkhuma, whose congregation was mostly from Assyrians of Urmia, was convinced that it was more advisable to stay in Iraq. He shared his opinion with his congregation saying: "The move is not to our advantage. In my opinion, moving to another Arab country and starting from scratch is not advisable. But people are free to make their own choices."

However, some Assyrian nationalists who were not members of the church; were spreading propaganda against the views of Pastor Khando. Also, those members of the congregation who were not in agreement with the views of the pastor were antagonized towards the ones who were.

Evil attempts were made to harm the pastor. One time a baked brick was thrown over his head from behind a wall. Another time, in a dispute, the opponents assaulted him. A third time ugly and shameful rumors were spread about him. Some evildoers instigated a low-class woman whose British husband had divorced her, to go to a judge and complain that the pastor on his way to the evening service, saw her sitting on a bench in the park (Hadiqa d'Ghazi). She claimed that he had come and pushed her from the bench knocking her to the ground.

The Arab judge who was in charge of the case did not believe the testimony of this wicked and lying woman. He advised Qasha Khando to open a case against her for attempted defamation of the pastor.

Of course, no one, including the opponents of the Qasha believed the false accusations against him. Qasha Khando did not open a case against this low-class woman. He said: "God is the judge and avenger of injustice. I will not sink to the level of this woman."

3-4 Assyrians of Urmia disguised as Ashirats, applied to move to Syria. But after a few years, they returned back to Iraq illegally. After they returned, they got into a lot of trouble with the Iraqi police.

# Chapter 14

## World Opinion Against the British Regarding the Plight of the Assyrians

A large number of newspapers accused the British government of granting independence to Iraq when it was not ready for it. Especially the British press was very critical of its own government.

Rev. William Wigram in a long speech addressed to the notables of an Asian assembly in England on October 23, 1933, praised the Assyrians for their loyal and unmatched contributions to the Allies during World War I and later on. He stated that the Assyrians, although a small nation, had assisted the Allies, especially the British beyond all expectations. The British owe them. They had promised to repatriate them to their ancestral homes. Instead, they made peace with Turkey and handed their homes and lands to Turkey. The British forgot the rights of this small and brave nation. They were enlisted in 1918 to give all to the Allied cause with promises by G.F. Gracy and other British officials. All the officers who have worked with the Assyrians attest to their bravery, capabilities, and dedication. They supported the Allies, especially the British. Therefore, he added, the British owe them and must find a solution for this nation to be settled in a safe place. He suggested that the participant governments in the Geneva Convention find a country for them.[17]

---

[17]    Translator's Note: In 1920, Wigram published a book titled "Our Smallest Ally" describing the role played by the small Assyrian nation during WWI.

General Dunsterville, the Commander in chief of the British army in Iran supported Dr. Wigram's proposal to find a home for the Assyrians. He suggested if possible, to ask Turkey to return the Highlands of Southern Kurdistan since they were included in The Turkish Tkhuma by mistake in 1925 when the boundaries between Turkey and Iraq were drawn under the direction of the Geneva Convention delegates. If necessary, England should buyback that territory.

R. S Stafford was the administrative inspector for Mosul. In his book The Assyrian Tragedy, he mentions the report he wrote regarding the Fesh-khabur and Dairabun incident. In this report, he states that when the Iraqi Dragon planes were bombing the Assyrians in Fesh-khabur in Northern Syria, the Assyrians were not counter-attacking because they thought they were British planes. According to Colonel Stafford on August 4, 1933, when the Assyrians re-crossed the river from Syria into Iraq with the purpose of surrendering to Iraqi forces in the Dairabun camp, regrettably some hot-headed ones panicked and opened fire on the camp.

This was a critical time for the Iraqi government. On the one hand, the Shia Muslims in the south of Diwaniya were in revolt against the Sunni-dominated government even though the Shiite were in the majority. On the other hand, King Faisal I had returned from Switzerland still sick, and dissatisfied with the actions of his ministers.

So, the real reason for the massacre of Assyrians was indifference to the condition of the Assyrians and the lack of correct governance on the part of the Iraqi officials.

After the unsuccessful attack of the Assyrians on the Iraqi

camp in Dairabun, a large number re-crossed the river back to Syria. Some were surrounded by the Iraqi Militia and killed in Dairabun. Around 200 climbed the mountain and reached their villages where they joined their families. Some surrendered their arms and were let go.

Colonel Stafford also notes that during the period of August 5-9, 1933 a dangerous anti-Assyrian propaganda campaign was spread claiming that armed Assyrians were amassing a force in the villages of southern Kurdistan plotting to attack the Iraqi army.

The frenzied Iraqi army became inflamed with the idea of exterminating all the Assyrians and getting rid of them once for all.

Even the civilian population in the villages was trying to help the army to annihilate the Assyrians. So, from August 7 on, they began to kill Assyrians here and there. Civilians around Dohuk were mercilessly murdered without having a case against them or brought for justice in the courts.

The number of civilians killed in Dohuk and environs reached 80. But the worst atrocity took place in Simele on August 11. Another mass extermination was planned to take place on August 13 in Alqosh because all Assyrians were included in the hatred campaign. But bne Alqosh were well-armed and ready to defend themselves.

Hikmat Sulayman, minister of the interior, the brother of Showkat Beg Sulayman, who was more Turk than Arab, was better than other Kurdish or Arab ministers. He came from Baghdad to Mosul and on August 11 had a meeting with the Ashirat tribal leaders. He advised them to tell their armed men to surrender their weapons to the government and end the bloodshed.

He had also arranged to have planes drop leaflets in all the villages calling the people to surrender their weapons to the Iraqi military posts. At that time he had no idea about the Simele Massacre because the news was not out yet. The next day Hikmat Sulayman went to Dohuk and Amadiya and subdued the skirmishes there. From there he went towards Simele, etc. On August 15 he returned to Mosul and informed Colonel Stafford about the dreadful tragedy that had taken place in Simele on August 11. He was greatly distressed by what he had witnessed.

A man by the name of Gibrael Yonan, the overseer of those areas, had tried to persuade the Assyrians of Simele not to be afraid because the government would protect them. He had hung his citizenship card around his neck and hung the Iraqi flag over his door-post. But the frenzied soldiers had torn his citizenship card and first killed him, then his son William.

According to Colonel Stafford's report, the number of individuals killed in Simele was 305 men, 4 women, and 6 children.

The government officials first claimed that the massacre was carried out by the various clans tribes.[18] This was, of course, a lie. Kurdish Bakir Sidqi, the commander of the whole army had commanded the massacre. His deputy commander of the Western regions of Iraq was an Arab by the name of Haji Ramadan.

---

[18] Translator's Note: Various Arab and Kurdish tribes in northern Iraq participated in the looting of the Assyrian villages.

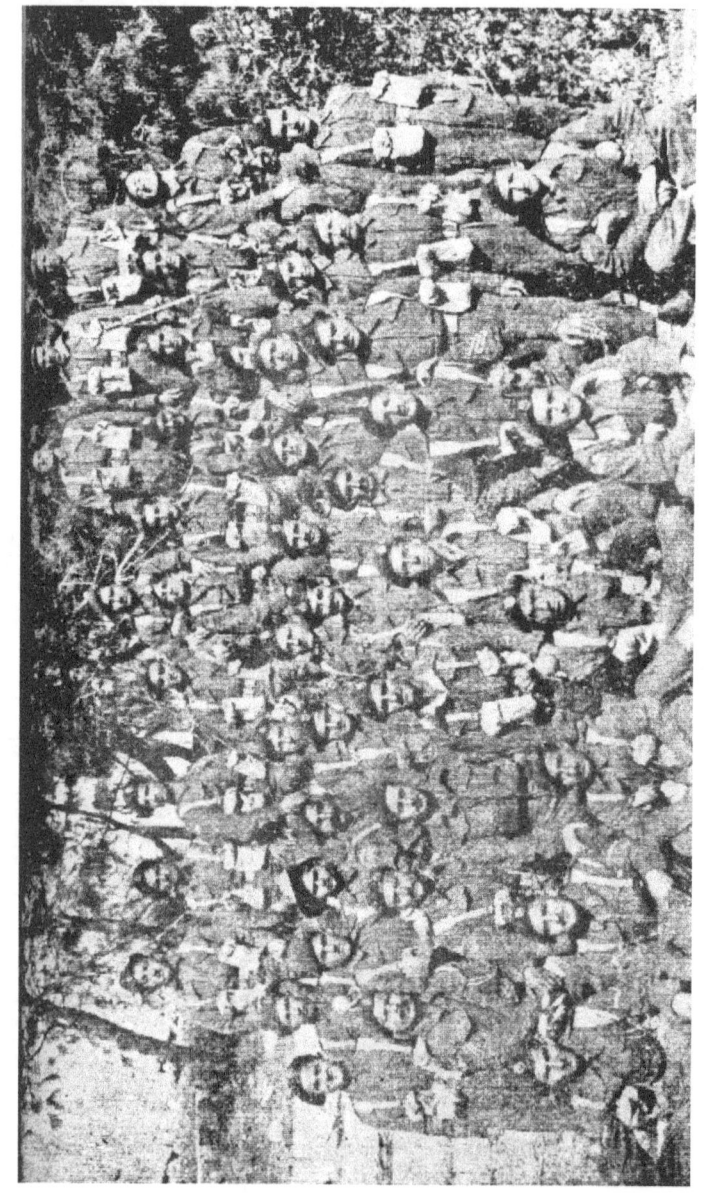

Assyrian Parachutists who landed behind the German Nazi Forces in Greece

Even though the Iraqi government tried to minimize or even deny the massacre, the Assyrians of Mosul very quickly spread the news worldwide first to the Beirut press then abroad even before the people in Mosul heard about it.

Now that the world had learned about the atrocities in Simele, Yasin Pasha, the Iraqi delegate in the League of Nations Peace Conference admitted that the Iraqi army was the culprit.

When Bakir Sidqi arrived in Baghdad he was greeted with a hero's welcome. He was seated beside high-ranking ministers, and the Crown Prince Ghazi bestowed a medal of victory to him in the absence of his father King Faisal I who was hospitalized in Switzerland a second time.

It is said that when Haji Ramadan rode into Mosul, the Arab women bent down and kissed the legs of his horse happy for having avenged their sons and men killed by the Assyrians.

According to Colonel Stafford, the total number of Assyrians killed in Simele, Zakho and Amadyia was 600. He stated that the majority of those who were killed had not been involved in the fights and were innocent citizens. 12 individuals were killed in a place called Suwara by the followers of Nisham Agha in Qala-d-Badreh near Dohuk. The total of those killed by the Kurds was 50. On the whole, the Kurds, except for looting, did not participate in the killings. On the contrary, there were instances when the Kurds tried to hide women and children to save their life.

One man by the name of Muhammad Agha from Garmavi stands out for decency and compassion in protecting Assyrians from pillage and murder.

The worst offender was Abdul Hamid Dabuni the mayor of Zakho. In contrast, the mayors Majid Beg of Amadiya, Aqra, Azra, Zibar, and Rawanduz were merciful towards the Assyrians that were in their administrative districts.

Also, the Arab tribes except for looting did not take part in the killings.

In Simele there was a police station headed by a Kurdish Sargent by the name of Naft Chavoush. He was initially a soldier in the Turkish army. He was not helpful, but the police under his supervision protected the Assyrian families.
The Simele massacre was a great stain on the history of Iraq when it was in its infancy.

As mentioned before, the news about the Assyrian massacre traveled via press in the whole world, especially in England. The British people prompted their government to find a solution to the plight of the Assyrians and find a safe country where they could relocate. There were proposals to move them to Brazil, Argentina, Canada, British Guyana, and other places.

An agency in England raised 250,000 Pounds for the expenses of relocation of the Assyrians.

Finally, the case of the homeless Assyrians was brought before the League of Nations. The petition was debated for a long time in the Geneva Convention. But as this was going on, the European skies were darkened by the clouds announcing the arrival of World War II. So the European powers focused on preparations for the Great War, and the Assyrian case was postponed to a later date.

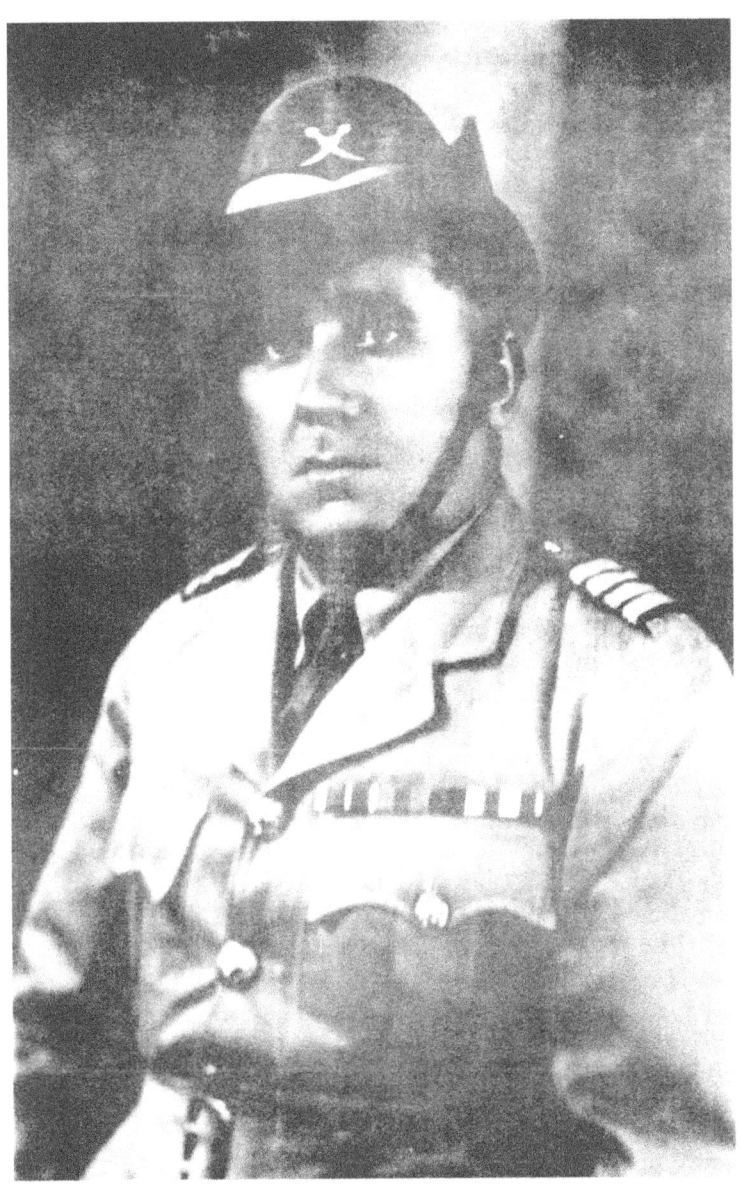

Major Zaya Gewargis the head of the Assyrian Military who
defeated Iraqi Army in Habbaniya

# Chapter 15

## World War II
## Its impact on the Middle Eastern
## Countries especially on the Assyrians

With the onset of World War II, the whole world fell into turmoil. Mr. Chamberlain, the British prime minister, made a treaty of non-aggression with the German leader Hitler. But the treaty lasted for one year only.

At the end of the year that is, September 1, 1939, the Germans attacked Poland. England and France sent an ultimatum to the Germans to stop attacking Poland otherwise they would attack Germany.

On the other hand, Russia attacked Poland as well. Italy went to war on the side of the Germans. Then, the USA became allied with England and France.

On October 7, 1941, the Japanese navy air force bombarded the American naval base in Pearl Harbor, on the Pacific Ocean. China joined the war on the side of the Allies that is, France, England, and the USA. (At that time China was not a communist country.)

Thus, World War II engulfed the whole world.

Once again, The British needed more fighters. They asked the Assyrians in Iraq and Syria to enlist in the Allied army. The Assyrians accepted the invitation and enlisted in the Allied force unconditionally.

From what I know, they served the Allies in Iraq, Iran, Palestine, Syria, and Cyprus. Some were trained as parachutists. They landed behind the enemy line in Greece and waged a surprise attack on the Germans. In a bloody battle, they took 90 German prisoners of war. King Paul of Greece gave the Assyrian parachutists a medal of honor for their agility and bravery. But 14 Assyrians were killed in that battle.

On May 2, 1941, the pro-German party under the Iraqi Prime Minister Rashid Ali al-Gaylani staged a successful coup against the royal family which included the young King Faisal II, his uncle Prince Abd al-Ellah, ruling for the underage Faisal II, and the whole family. The royal family fled to Basra and from there they boarded a ship and stayed on board to see what would happen in the country.

Rashid Ali became very powerful and sent a large army to Habbaniya. The British had a small garrison of levies and a few airplanes at that base. The levies were composed of mostly Assyrians with a smaller number of Kurds and Yezidis. A fierce battle took place between these two forces. In the beginning, the British lost hope and intended to surrender to the enemy. But the Assyrians said they would fight to the last man and would not surrender to the Arabs. So they persisted and the Arab army was defeated by this small force in Habbaniya. The Arabs began to run away and the Assyrians went in pursuit until the village of Fallujah. They even entered the village after them. Later we heard that the inhabitants had complained that the Assyrians entered their homes, looted some property, and killed some soldiers. We do not know to what extent this is true.

Rashid Ali escaped to Iran before the return of the royal family to Baghdad because undoubtedly he would have been punished.

In 1945 World War II ended. The world took a breath. The European countries and others suffered greatly from hunger, thirst, and loss of life. Houses were in ruin; cities were destroyed.

Nations began to recuperate from war. Slowly they started reconstruction and living in peace each in their own country.

We the Assyrians living in Iraq began to forget the worries and fears we had due to the instability of political conditions in the country during the years of persecutions and war. We began to move forward with our lives and occupations. The Arabs of Iraq too began to forget the animosity between us and them during the years of instability in the country and we began to live in friendship and peace as members of one nation.

At that time conditions in the country of Iran, like the other countries, were not stable. Even though the Allied forces were still in the central and southern regions of the country, they honored their policy of non-interference in the affairs of the country, and soon withdrew their forces completely from Iran.

But the Soviet army which had occupied the western and northern parts of the country such as Azerbaijan, etc., lingered on for a long time. They did not pull their forces out of the country as the others did. Their stay planted the seeds of discord and communist ideology among the inhabitants of the region. The Soviet plan was to spread their ideology in that area.

The Allies urged the Soviets to evacuate Azerbaijan immediately since they had no reason to stay there any longer. So, they were forced to pull out. But as I said, they left behind a microbe or a destructive seed against the governing regime.

Hardly out of Iran, a rebel by the name of Ja'far Pishevari, a Afshar, [native Turk] staged a coup with his gang of followers against the government and created a secessionist state in Azerbaijan.

The majority of Azerbaijanis are Afshars. They are not Persians. Pishevari took this bold step with the help of the Soviets. The goal of the Soviets was to create a separate enclave called "the Democrats" in Azerbaijan and annex it to Soviet Azerbaijan which Russia had separated from Iran when Tsar Nicolai was the emperor of Russia.

At the same time, the Kurds to the west of Azerbaijan, an area on the border of Iran and Turkey, created an independent state called the Democratic Republic of Kurdistan.

The Assyrians of Urmia and Salamas were caught in a political whirlwind. They were afraid of their Muslim neighbors. They were also caught between two different political standpoints. One part supported the central Iranian government; while the other aspired to have their own autonomous republic.

As mentioned before, the Soviets had not evacuated the region completely. As you know, our people tend to be won over easily without assessing deeply the future consequences of their decisions. Also, they were still loyal to the Russians even though these Russians were not the same as the former ones.

Some people in the villages were led to believe they would be exempt from paying taxes to the landlords. They were thinking since the land belonged to them, why should they pay a land tax to the landlord? Every day they were bombarded with speeches on such issues. So these naïve peasants became members of the political party called "Hezb-e-Tudeh" [Tudeh Party] not knowing this was a new name for communists.

There was an Assyrian man from the village of Ada by the name of Esho Piraley. I think he had come from Russia. He was an ordinary middle-aged man. He started a propaganda campaign against paying land tax to the landlords and such. After winning the opinion of some of the people, he put together a band of followers especially from those villages that were on the slopes neighboring the Kurdish mountains. Thus a group of peasants, their machine guns on their shoulders, marched in front of this person visiting other villages and the town of Urmia extracting money donations from townspeople, and at times, threatening them.

Then Mr. Piraley brought 15-20 armed Kurds and forced homeowners to feed them, prepare individual bedding for them, and give them pocket money for other expenses of those Kurds.

He made a long list of the Assyrians who were opposed to the actions of this group and were loyal to the central government. They were assassinated one by one to advance his satanic schemes. Thus he carried out his scheme by singling out individuals and terrorizing them. First, his gang wounded a young man named Shimshun of Charbash who died shortly after. The second person was Mirza Yoel of Charbash who was assassinated in front of the door of his house. He was a prominent person in both the Assyrian and Muslim communities and was a pro-government sympathizer in Urmia. Then they assassinated Hakim Alexan, the son of Nazrakhan. He was a well-known and highly respected person not only among the Assyrians but also in the government circles. He had friends among notable Iranians. They assassinated a dentist by the name of Baba. He was from Charbash too. Then the head of the police force, Valizadeh was assassinated. They shot and killed him in his office.

They had created a reign of terror in the town of Urmia. When the Soviets learned about the long list of assassinations, they realized their plans might backfire. They intervened. Esho Piraley disappeared from view. Until now no one knows what the end of this man was.

In 1945 the Iranian army was well-trained and equipped with new weapons. A large force invaded Tabriz, the capital of the Tudeh regime, and defeated Pishevari's weak force. His army was scattered and totally destroyed. He fled to the Russian Caucasus. Later we learned that he died in a car accident.

The Iranian army entered Azerbaijan and punished those who had participated in the Tudeh uprisings during those months. According to a man from Charbash, the rebels were run over by army tanks. Some of the Assyrians in this group were Awraham Yangeeja, Aram Aprim, khosrov Mando and others.

As we found out later, the Charbash Assyrians were more sympathetic to the Soviets than others.

Once again, in 1946 the village of Charbash was plundered as reported by the aforementioned person.

A man by the name of Rabi Youshiya was arrested and tried. Then he was hanged in the town center. This was at the same time that the Iranian army was punishing the Tudeh rebels.

There was a group of Assyrians who were involved with the Tudeh political party. In fear of being arrested, they fled through the mountains of Kurdistan and arrived in Baghdad. They stayed in Iraq until the king of Iran granted all of them amnesty to return to Iran. Some returned to Urmia; but others took Iraqi citizenship and stayed in Iraq.

As mentioned before, the conditions in Iraq after World War II began to stabilize. But in July 14, 1958 all of a sudden a strange political wave brought great transformations in Iraq. Some military leaders staged a coup against the king. The young King Faisal II with his uncle Abd al-Ellah and some members of the family were assassinated. A large number of the government ministers such as Nuri Pasha, who as the prime minister had run the affairs of the country for many years, was arrested and shamefully paraded in the streets of Baghdad before being killed. Some of his cabinet members were also arrested, tried, and sent to jail.

For 7-8 years, different groups changed power in Iraq; one political party rising against, and replacing another.

So, as years went by, due to the recurrent turmoil and upheavals in Iraq, our people began to search for a safe haven to ensure the future of our nation.

They appealed to the World Council of Churches.

Consequently, the United States of America opened its doors to our people to immigrate to this large and prosperous country. There are now approximately 50,000 Assyrians who live and partake in the blessings of this country. Of course, there are about 100,000 in other countries such as England, Canada, Australia, France, Sweden, and other parts of the world. No less than 200,000 are still in Iraq and some thousands are in Iran. Thousands of others live in Lebanon and Syria.

This has been the destiny of our people. We have been scattered in the four corners of the world much as the Israelites were some 20 centuries ago when God punished them and scattered them in foreign lands.

Today the most important goal of the Assyrians as a nation is to return to the Lord and ask Him to help us to return to our first love, to the faith that our renowned forefathers had, and for Him to be our Lord and the king in our life. To ask Him to raise individuals in our nation to work for a brighter future for our nation that has been through so much tribulation and has suffered many persecutions in years past.
Amen.

I offer my gratitude to the Lord
Who, in my old age, enabled me
To accomplish in writing
This history for a gift to my people.

# Postscript

The book by Rabi Koorish provides a new and clearer view of the events that took place during this century which was the most bitter in the history of the Assyrian people.

Rabi Koorish was an eyewitness to the events that he describes in this historical account.

Most other writers have based their writings on hearsay from others who have a tendency to add or subtract from what they have heard. They have not had the ability to sift the truth from what they have heard. But everything that Rabi Koorish has written is based on truth.

We owe him a great debt for this work. We are aware of the great value and benefit that he has offered us in this book. We have learned new, and unforgettable lessons that help us build a better future for the present Assyrians and those who will come after them.

Shamasha Gewargis-d-bet Benyamin

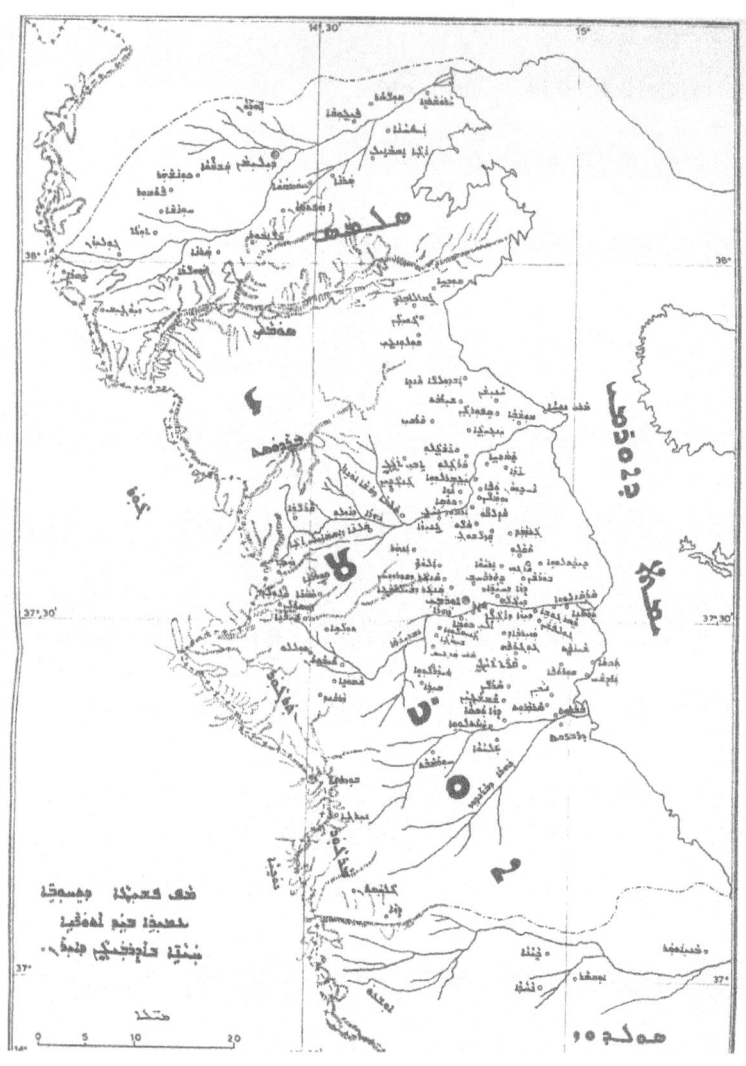

Map depicting the boundaries where the Assyrians lived in Azerbaijan, Iran

www.ingramcontent.com/pod-product-compliance
Lightning Source LLC
Chambersburg PA
CBHW051215170526
45166CB00005B/1909

* 9 7 8 1 4 7 0 9 4 9 6 3 1 *